I0446388

The Art of Teen Finance:

Crafting Your Financial Future

Written

By: Daniel Uribe M.A.S.E.P.

"Formal Education will make you a Living…but Self-Education will make you a Fortune."
-Jim Rohn

Preface

Welcome to "The Art of Teen Finance: Crafting Your Financial Future." In the vast landscape of personal finance literature, this book stands as a unique guide, specially tailored for teenagers seeking to navigate the intricate world of money management. As you embark on this journey, you'll discover that financial success is not only achievable but can be an empowering and enriching experience.

In a world where financial literacy is often overlooked in traditional education, this book aims to fill the gap by providing practical insights, valuable lessons, and actionable strategies designed specifically for teens. Money, though often seen as a complex and daunting subject, is, at its core, a tool that, when wielded with knowledge and responsibility, can shape a future of independence and abundance.

"The Art of Teen Finance" is more than just a manual on budgeting, saving, and investing. It's a holistic exploration of the financial landscape, covering topics such as understanding the value of money, making informed spending decisions, and setting realistic financial goals. Through relatable examples, real-life stories, and interactive exercises, this book seeks to empower teens to make informed financial choices that align with their aspirations.

Crafting your financial future is, indeed, an art. It requires creativity, discipline, and a willingness to learn. This book is your brush, and the canvas is your financial journey. Each chapter is a stroke, building a masterpiece of financial wisdom and acumen.

As you delve into the pages that follow, remember that your financial education is a lifelong process. "The Art of Teen Finance" is here to provide you with a solid foundation, equipping you with the knowledge and skills needed to shape your financial destiny. Embrace the journey, ask questions, and, most importantly, apply what you learn. Your financial future is yours to craft, and with the right tools, it can be a masterpiece.

Here's to your financial success and the artistry of crafting a future filled with prosperity, security, and abundance.

TABLE OF CONTENTS

4. Overleveraging Loans & Interest: "With the Cost of Living Rising Each and Every Year, Borrowing Money in the Form of Loans and Credit is Becoming a Normal Part of Everyday Life."

5. Paying Uncle Sam: "Back in the year 1789, Benjamin Franklin, one of the Founding Fathers of the United States of America, once said there are only two things Certain in Life…Death and Taxes."

Phase Two: Financial Stability

6. Differentiating Between Income & Expenses: "If you don't Focus on Understanding how Money Flows in and out of your hands you will be on a path headed straight for Financial Disaster."

7. Learning How to Budget: "How Useful is Learning how to Make a Lot of Money if you Never Learn How to Keep it?"

8. Choosing Between Leasing & Owning: "Should I Buy a Home, or Rent an Apartment? Should I Buy a Car or Lease a Car?"

9. Investing in Bonds: "By Investing in a Bond, you Become the one Loaning Money to the Federal Government and the Federal Government in return pays you Interest for having Loaned them that Money."

10. Contributing to Your 401K: "The Vast Majority of individuals don't have the Slightest Clue as to how much Money they actually need to Save in order to Retire and Maintain a Good Quality of Life."

Phase Three: Financial Security

11. Understanding Inflation: "I remember when I was a kid gas was $0.69 cents a Gallon and we could Fill up a Tank of Gas with just Ten Bucks"

12. Differentiating between Assets & Liabilities: "Many people go through life with very little Financial Education and make the critical mistake of Buying Liabilities that they believe are Assets."

13. Choosing Profits Over Wages: "We're Groomed from a very young age to Become Good Employees rather than Become Good Investors and Entrepreneurs."

14. The Meaning of being Rich vs Wealthy: "Many of us grow up Idolizing Professional Athletes, Famous Celebrities, Movie Actors and Actresses, and Music Artists because of their Fame but even more so because of their Fortune."

15. Opportunity During Recession: "One of the most Famous quotes made by Arguably the Greatest Investor of All Time, Warren Buffet... "Be Fearful when others are Greedy, and Greedy when others are Fearful."

Phase Four: Financial Freedom & Abundance

16. Creating Multiple Streams of Income: "By Leveraging these Devices and the Accessibility of the Online World, you can very Easily Learn to Make Money from the Comfort of your Own Home."

17. Investing in the Stock Market: "General Rule of Thumb you should always remember…If it Sounds too Good to be True, it probably is."

18. Investing in the Real Estate Market: "It's Estimated that Over the Course of the last two hundred years, over 90% percent of the World's Millionaires have been created by Investing in Real Estate."

19. The Power of Compound Interest: "The Concept of Compounding is often Compared to what's known as The Snowball Effect."

20. Learning How to Create Assets: "When Individuals Learn how to Create Assets, they

have in Essence, learned how to Build their Own Money Printing Machine."

21. Escaping the Rat Race: "We are now able to Detach ourselves from the day-to-day Grind allowing us to have the Ultimate and most Prized Reward of all…Freedom of Time."

Phase 1: Financial Survival

Individuals in the phase of financial survival:

- [ ] Are making minimum wage.
- [ ] Can hardly afford to make ends meet at the end of every month.
- [ ] Feel powerless, frustrated, anger, and shame for the financial circumstances they are in.
- [ ] Place all the blame on employers, parents, family, and their upbringing for not being able to make more money.

DEFINING MONEY & VALUE

"EVERY INTERACTION IN YOUR LIFE INVOLVING MONEY HAS SHAPED THE WAY YOU VIEW AND PERCEIVE MONEY"

From the time you were a kid, all through your adolescence, and now being a young adult, you've been learning both consciously and unconsciously about how the world works and why it works the way that it does. Whether you've had conversations with your friends about the healthcare system in the United States, watched YouTube videos about the sun and our solar system, or read books about the ancient Egyptians and how they built massive pyramids, your brain is constantly taking information in and storing it in different areas which enables you to form some unique perception about why the world is the way it is.

The concept of "Money" is no different from any of the other concept or idea you've ever learned about. Every interaction in your life up to this point involving money has shaped the way you view and perceive money. But how do you know if you're perception of money is correct? Isn't everyone's view of money the same? And isn't the value of money the same for everyone? If you've ever wondered why some people make a lot of money, why some people make very little money, why some people spend all of their money, and why others save their money...the answer lies in the way these individuals THINK about money. Your thoughts are at the very root of everything that has ever manifested in your life.

Before we dive too deep into anything else, let's first come to a very basic and common understating of what money actually is and why money has value (if any at all).

Definitions & Examples

Money: A circulating medium of exchange including coins, paper money, and demand deposits.

Value: The worth of something in terms of the amount of other things for which it can be exchanged or in terms of some medium of exchange.

Example 1.

When you go to Starbucks to get your morning Latte the attendant at the cash register will ask you for some form of payment in exchange for your Latte. You'll usually have the option to either pay in cash, coins, debit or credit card, using gift cards, and now and days even digital wallets such as Apple and Google Pay.

Now, to connect the dots in terms of money and value in the example given above...you are willing to pay let's say $4.25 (four dollars and twenty-five cents) for a Latte because you perceive $4.25 of value in the beverage being given to you. The value you assign to it depends solely on your perspective. Maybe the Latte allows you to show up to school or work more alert and you're able to be more productive, or maybe you only buy Lattes every so often and simply feel a need to satisfy your craving. And from YOUR perspective you're willing to pay $4.25 worth of money in exchange for these benefits. If Starbucks decided to double the price and now the same beverage would cost you $8.50, would you still be willing to buy it?

For those of you who see eight dollars and fifty cents of value the answer is yes, and for those of you who don't see eight dollars and fifty cents worth of value the answer is no. For those of you who don't even drink coffee or think Starbucks is too expensive to begin with, you likely don't see any value in buying a Latte in the morning even if they decreased their prices. Which again is attributed to the value you assign to it, if it doesn't provide $4.25 worth of value in your life it's very likely you won't purchase it. The same goes for every single purchase you will make in your entire life. Does the product or service you are purchasing provide enough value for you that you are willing to pay the selling price? That is a key point to understand when you are on the flip side (building your own business) which we'll get into in a later section.

Money Myths
"Money can't Buy Happiness."
- Although it's true money cannot buy happiness, it doesn't mean that individuals who have money are sad and depressed. Or in other words, individuals can have a lot of money and be happy in exactly the way individuals can have very little money and be happy. Money in general doesn't determine your level of happiness, although it does give you an increasingly amount of options that may make your life easier, and possibly more enjoyable.

"Money is the Root of all Evil."

- Money is not the root of all that is evil, and that perspective seems to be rather extreme. Money can be used for good causes: funding treatment for cancer research, funding community housing, funding youth centers, grants, scholarships, you name it. And from a more individualized perspective, one can suggest that in actuality money amplifies the character of whom the person already is. If a person is greedy, they are greedy with or without money. If a person is generous, they're generous with or without money.

"All Rich people are Greedy."

- Simply not true. There are just as many greedy people who aren't rich as there are greedy people who are rich. There are a multitude of millionaires and billionaires that consistently give back to the community and genuinely do their best to provide value in the marketplace. It's not always about being greedy and making money for individuals with plentiful financial resources.

Self-Reflection

1. What are some of the misconceptions about money you've been told that you feel have negatively impacted the way you think and feel about money?

2. Using the definitions of money and value given in this section, what is something you have purchased that you feel was overpriced? What benefits did this product or service promise but fail to deliver?

3. Using the definitions of money and value given in this section, what is something you have purchased that you feel was underpriced? What benefits did this product or service promise and over deliver?

CONTROLLING YOUR CREDIT SCORE

"NEVER WILL YOU BE ASKED BY A FINANCING REPRESENTATIVE WHAT YOUR GPA WAS IN HIGH SCHOOL, WHAT YOUR SAT SCORES WERE, WHETHER OR NOT YOU PASSED YOUR ENGLISH LITERATURE TEST, OR WHAT KIND OF EXTRACURRICULAR ACTIVITIES YOU TOOK PART IN AFTER SCHOOL"

If you're ever looking to get financing to buy yourself a new car, buy your first home, rent your first apartment, or take out a loan to attend college or university to further your education, you will without a doubt be asked…"What does your credit score look like?" It's literally one of the most important numbers you'll need to track and keep up with as an adult. Never will you be asked by a sales or financing representative what your GPA was in high school, what your SAT scores were, whether or not you passed your English Literature test, or what kind of extracurricular activities you took part in after school. Without sugar coating it, those things simply don't matter when it comes to getting approved for credit or a loan.

Now, most individuals eventually get a decent enough grip and semi-understand how their credit score can affect their financial decisions and in a more overall sense their life, but usually this understanding comes with a ton of mistakes in early adulthood. This is easily explainable. When we're young, we're not thinking about buying a house, we're not thinking about raising a family, we're not thinking about retirement, we're not thinking about how debt affects our finances, and we don't put much thought into the importance of our credit score and how it will have an impact in all of these aspects of our lives.

Because of this, many of us have to spend years and years re-adjusting our financial habits in order to build our credit score up high enough to be at a healthy level and thus to work in our benefit. Which at the end of the day is okay, there's absolutely nothing wrong with learning from trial and error. What we must consider however is how our financial futures can be drastically different if we instead learn about credit early on and make good financial decisions right from the get go. Not only would we set ourselves up to save and make a lot more money, but we would also set ourselves up to use leverage (time and money) to exponentially increase our income potential.

Definition & Examples

Credit Score: your credit score is a three-digit number ranging from 300 to 850 that tells someone the likelihood of you being able to pay back the debt you have acquired.

A score of 300 is considered a very poor/low score and a score of 850 is considered an exceptional/perfect score.

Example 1.

Johnny is a week away from graduating high school, and as an early graduation gift his parents decide to buy him a brand-new car. It's a four door 2023 Honda Accord, silver just like Johnny wanted, he's absolutely ecstatic and can't wait to show it off to all his friends. Before he does however, Johnny feels a need to add some finishing touches to help his car "stand-out" from the crowd. So he goes to an auto accessories shop the very next day and inquires about adding a top of the line stereo system, limousine tint for all four windows, and twenty inch chrome rims with new tires. The sales representative happily helps him and hands Johnny the quote for all the items he is requesting:

New Stereo System: $600

Limousine Tint: $160

Chrome Rims: $900

Tires for new Rims: $800:

Installation for all items: $300

Grand Total: $2,760

Johnny has only been able to save up about $250 from the weekly allowance he's being given by his parents and plans to get a job right after his high school graduation. The sales representative explains that they can help him finance this purchase with zero money down, but only if Johnny's credit score is above 600. Johnny has never made this type of a purchase before and has no clue what his credit score is or how it works. The sales representative runs Johnny's credit, comes back and tells him his credit score is too low and won't be able to get approved for this purchase unless he brings someone else with him that has a good credit score to co-sign on the loan with him.

Having a good credit score pays in the long run and helps you be more in control of your financial decisions. Again, your score is simply a numerical value that tells someone how responsible you are of paying back debt. Now, when you're trying to finance a purchase and have someone "run your credit," what that usually means is that they are pulling up your credit information and returning with an overall FICO score. FICO (a data analytics company) scores are the most commonly used score by banks and financial institutions when it comes to determining whether or not they can approve you. And because this is such an important score, you should have a firm understanding as to how your score is calculated. Overall, your FICO score is divided into five different categories or components each having a distinct impact on your overall score. Here's what those categories are:

Your payment history: has a 35% impact on your score

The amount that you owe: has a 30% impact in your score

Length of your credit history: has a 15% impact on your score

New Credit: has a 10% impact on your score

Credit Mix: has a 10% impact on your score

From this list, you can see why someone who pays all of their bills on time, owes very little on other loans and credit, has had open credit accounts for many years, doesn't constantly open new credit accounts, and has a good credit mix (credit card, mortgage, business loan) will have a higher credit score than someone who never pays their bills on time, owes a lot of money to his/her creditors, has had a relatively short credit history, is constantly opening up new credit accounts, and doesn't have a good credit mix. It may sound difficult at first, but having and maintaining an overall good credit score is actually fairly simple. The trick is making a conscious effort in learning what constitutes a good score, and implementing that criteria into all the financial decisions you make each and every day. By making sound financial decisions each and every day your credit score will automatically be on the rise, and you'll have a perfect score before you know it.

Money Myths

"You can have bad Credit and still get approved for a loan."

-Yes, this is true, however you'd be setting yourself up for failure if you took out a loan with bad credit. How so? In general, the better your credit score is the better interest rate the lending company will be willing to offer you. And the opposite is true about having a bad credit score, the lower your credit score the higher interest rate the lending company will offer you. At the end of the day the lending company wants to get paid and make a profit from the money they lend you, and the better your credit score is the more likely you are to repay that loan (from a lending company perspective). Taking out a loan on bad credit and having a high interest rate on that loan makes it more difficult to pay back, and all the money you'd be paying in interest would be equivalent to taking cash and lighting it on fire. Simply a waste!

"In order to build up my Credit Score I should buy a lot of stuff on credit."

- In a literal sense yes this is true, however I wouldn't recommend it. A lot of individuals go out and buy jewelry, clothes, shoes, and accessories with a credit card and make minimum payments when the bill arrives. And there is nothing morally wrong with doing this, but financially speaking there are reasons why not to make these sorts of purchases. One, you're buying luxuries instead of necessities. If instead you bought gas and food for example and put those on a credit card, those are things you would need to buy anyway and often times credit cards offer rewards or cash back for these purchases. Secondly, by making minimum payments you're having to pay interest every month, which again is similar to getting lighter fluid and setting your cash on fire.

Self-Reflection

1. What sorts of purchases can you make to help improve your credit score?

2. What can you do to avoid falling into the credit trap causing your credit score to suffer?

3. Why do you believe some individuals are not able to limit, or moderate their spending?

THE CREDIT CARD TRAP

"THE MENTALITY OF "I'LL JUST PAY FOR IT LATER" OR "I'LL JUST MAKE THE MINIMUM PAYMENTS" CAN AND WILL LAND MOST OF US IN A DEBT TRAP THAT CAN BE EXTREMELY DIFFICULT TO DIG OURSELVES OUT OF."

Now that you have a better understanding about credit scores and how those are calculated, let's take a look at another huge problem in the United States: credit cards. It's estimated that the average household in America carries an average credit card debt of approximately $7,900, which is significant to say the least. How does this happen? Well, the truth is that it's very easy to go out shopping, eat at fancy restaurants, take extravagant vacations, and party all night with friends and pay for everything by simply swiping a piece of plastic. The mentality of "Oh I'll just pay for it later" or "I'll just make the minimum payments" can and will land most of us in a debt trap that can be extremely difficult to dig ourselves out of. Not to mention that credit card fees and the interest rates on credit cards are some of the highest across the entire financial industry.

Credit cards, in a sense, give us the ability to finance a lifestyle that we can't actually afford. Let's be honest, if we could actually afford to go shopping for clothes every weekend, eat at fancy restaurants, take amazing vacations, and party with friends at the club every Friday and Saturday night, then we should be able to pay for everything with cash...right? When we can actually afford the items we buy we should be able to pay in cash, and not even have to think twice about it. But instead, we use credit cards, max those credit cards out meaning we spend $1,000, $2,000. $3,000 dollars, and then make the minimum $25 payments at the end of every billing cycle and believe we're living a life we can actually afford. But that couldn't be further from the truth.

Definitions & Examples

Credit Card: a payment card given to users that allows the cardholder to pay for goods and services. The cardholder has an agreement however to pay the card issuer for those amounts in addition to other agreed charges.

Example 1.

Paula just got a new job at a nearby restaurant as a server and is excited to finally start making some money. Before she gets her first paycheck she goes to Chase bank, where she has her checking account, in order to open up a savings account. That way she can begin putting money in her savings every other week as she gets paid and earns tips. As she's at Chase opening up her new account, the representative she's speaking with asks her if she's interested in receiving a Chase credit card that offers 0% APR (Annual Percentage Rate) for the first 6 months? Paula doesn't have any credit cards at the moment, and is excited about an offer that involves zero percent interest. She happily accepts the generous offer, and the credit card is mailed to her home the very next week.

Annual Percentage Rate (APR): a measure of the cost of the credit that you will be carrying, measured as a yearly rate.

Example 2.

Paula gets her credit card and begins buying items ahead of her paychecks. She isn't being charged any interest and wants to take full advantage. Three, four, five months pass and Paula still hasn't made a single payment to Chase bank. Before she realizes it, the seventh month arrives, and she finally plans to make her first payment. As she opens up her bill she's shocked at what her balance is: $1,345 (one thousand, three hundred, and forty five dollars).

She doesn't have enough money to pay off her entire balance and sees that the minimum payment is only $35 dollars, which is great! Her eyes continue to scroll down her bill, and she notices the Annual Percentage Rate for her card is listed at 24.99% after the initial first six months. What does that mean in terms of actual money?

$1,345 (total balance) x 0.2499 (annual percentage rate) = $336.12 (total interest)

It means that Paula will end up owing an additional $336.12 (three hundred and thirty six dollars and twelve cents) in interest. That's a grand total of:

$1,345 (total balance) + $336.12 (total interest) = $1,681.12 (new total balance)

One thousand, six hundred, and eighty one dollars with twelve cents is her new total balance! And it can continue to rise higher and higher if she continues with her same spending habits, spending more than what she can actually afford to pay back.

What should be becoming increasingly clear in your mind is that banks, lenders, and financial institutions make a huge amount of profit from keeping you in debt! The more debt you ultimately carry, the more of your hard earned money you'll be handing over to your creditors in the form of interest. It's no coincidence that as you get older and make more money you'll randomly get letters mailed to your home from different banks and credit unions offering you credit cards filled with perks and zero percent interest for the first few months. They're simply offering you products and making it as easy as possible for you to spend more and more money that you actually don't have. You're literally playing in an ugly financial figame, and being set up to lose.

Are using credit cards always a bad idea? Well, that's debatable, even amongst millionaires and billionaires. Some will argue that if you plan on being rich one day you should stop using credit cards at all costs, and others will say it's okay to use credit cards as long as you have the money to pay off the entire balance when the bill arrives. Clearly, both points of view take into account how dangerous credit cards can be and how quickly your debt can get out of control. I would argue that using credit cards is okay, as long as you're using them to purchase items you would have to purchase anyway like groceries and gas. Most credit cards will offer 1%-5% percent cash back on items like groceries and gas, which will allow you to earn at least a small percentage of you money back. You should most definitely however be able to pay your bill by the deadline posted, otherwise, you'll be paying back a high rate of interest and making your creditors rich instead of making yourself rich.

Money Myths
"It's important to have credit cards in case of an emergency"
- Although credit can be leveraged as cash in the event of a financial emergency, what the priority should really be is having cash at your disposal. We should all have a certain amount of cash in our savings account to use when needed, not credit cards. It's also important to distinguish between what an emergency and a non-emergency entail. Suffering from serious injuries requiring medical attention would

definitely qualify as an emergency, but would being stressed out from work and "needing" to take a vacation to Miami also qualify? Not really. Not that there's anything wrong with going to Miami it's a beautiful destination, but if you need to use credit cards to pay for your trip you should probably look for more affordable destinations.

"It's important to carry a balance on multiple credit cards in order to build up your credit score"
- We have to be careful here. Although having a good credit mix is important to building up your overall score, you're score will also decrease if you're constantly inquiring for new credit. In addition, we also must be careful with the psychological effects having multiple credit cards can have on an individual. If we have three credit cards each having a limit of $1,500, we may feel like we have access to $4,500 dollars which would entice us to spend more and more, but again that's actually not the case.

Self-Reflection
1. What can you do to avoid paying credit card fees and interest?

2. Are there any instances when maxing out credit cards is a good idea as a consumer? Are there any instances when maxing out credit cards is a good idea as a business owner? Why or why not?

OVERLEVERAGING LOANS & INTEREST

"WITH THE COST OF LIVING RISING EACH AND EVERY YEAR, BORROWING MONEY IN THE FORM OF LOANS AND CREDIT IS BECOMING A NORMAL PART OF EVERYDAY LIFE."

It's very important to understand loans and interest especially when we're considering life in the modern era. Why? With cost of living rising each and every year, borrowing money in the form of loans and credit from banks and financial institutions and paying interest on these personal and credit loans is becoming a normal part of everyday life. Simply put, we need more money to live and keep up with the steady increase in prices that seemingly continue to rise with no end in sight (gas, housing, food). Let's give you a glimpse to some statistics so you can see some of the staggering debt figures in the United States:

- The average college graduate has a student loan debt of $37,000.

- The average consumer has a total car debt equal to $31,000.
- The average amount of money spent on a wedding is $26,000.
- The average homeowner has a mortgage debt equal to $200,000.
- The average cost of raising a child through the age of 17 is approximately $233,000.

These numbers are scary, but can be even higher depending in what state and city you live in (it's even more expensive to live in big metropolitan areas such as New York City, Los Angeles, and San Francisco). Still think money isn't important?

Definitions & Examples

Loan: the act of lending on condition of being returned.

Interest Rate: an amount charged on top of the principal by a lender to a borrower.

Example 1.

John is on the brink of graduating high school and the only thing on his mind is moving out and marrying his high school sweetheart and love of his life Mary. They have been together since their freshmen year and feel they are more than ready to tie the knot.

John has been working part-time his senior year as a sales associate at Foot Locker and now plans on working full-time to save more money. Up to this point he's been able to save a grand total of $2,200, which he is ecstatic about. Also, John and Mary's parents have agreed to contribute a combined total of $5,000 to help with the wedding expenses, which is a huge help.

John and Mary begin to plan out their wedding and quickly come to the realization that they may not be able to have the big, beautiful, extravagant wedding they both had visualized in their mind for so long. So far, these are what the wedding expenses look like:

- Wedding ring and bands- $4,000
- Venue & Decorations- $3,000
- Food and Beverages (for 100 guests)- $2,500
- Wedding Dress and Tuxedo- $1,300
- Honey Moon (Hawaii for a week)- $3,000
- Photo & Videographer- $1,500

- Bridal Shower, Bachelor & Bachelorette Party- $1,700
- DJ and live Entertainment- $1,100

Which brings us to a grand total of $18,100!!! And again, all expenses are still not accounted for. Instead of waiting for a few more years to save up for the remaining $10,900 still needed for the wedding....
$18,100 (total wedding cost) − $7,200 (total money saved) = $10,900 (total money still needed)
.... they decide to take out two personal loans amounting to $20,000 at a 12% interest rate in order to pay for their wedding.

Is taking out two personal loans to pay for wedding expenses the right move? Or are there other options that should've received more consideration? On one hand, people have the legal and moral right to spend money in whatever way they want on whatever it is they want. But, from a strictly financial perspective, taking out two personal loans with high interest rates to pay for something that will have absolutely no financial return in the long run doesn't make much sense. Not to mention that all the money spent on the wedding will be blown on one single day!

And not only is it a bad financial decision, but it's the wrong way to start off a long-term relationship (building bad financial habits!).

It's important to keep the big picture in mind. Instead of seeking the immediate satisfaction of taking out loans and paying interest to buy luxuries like extravagant weddings, fancy cars, and nice accessories, the priority should be to be debt free so not to have a burden on your shoulders and being stuck in a huge financial hole. Professional athletes and entertainers do this all the time, which is why you always hear about someone who makes a ton of money going broke and filing for bankruptcy. When someone who has bad financial habits suddenly is given millions of dollars, you can be positively sure they will spend it just as quickly as the money came into their hands. However, when someone who has exceptional financial habits is suddenly given millions of dollars the opposite will be true. They will be sure to save and invest, which in the long run will allow them to make more money.

Money Myths

"Don't worry about paying off your debt just make the minimum payments."

- False. If you ever want to be debt free and prosper financially you should absolutely prioritize paying off your debt and not just making the minimum payment posted on your bill. Having lingering debt will feel like you have a huge weight on your shoulders that will only continue to get heavier the more you finance your lifestyle.

"You should take out a personal loan to pay off your other debts."

- In extreme situations this might be your only option, however you should always try your best to avoid taking out loans to pay off other loans. By doing this you're just like Picking your Poison, which at the end of the day doesn't do you any good. Instead, what you should do is analyze your expenses and see what expenditures you can decrease that will free up some cash you can then allocate to paying off your debt. If you're having trouble paying off your debt yet are partying every weekend, then you have a money management problem and not a cash flow problem.

"Don't worry about paying interest."

- To be financially successful you need to develop a Love/Hate relationship with the concept of interest. With every ounce of your body, you should Hate paying your lender interest every month, and with every ounce of your body you should Love being paid interest by your borrowers every month. Again, the premise of this entire book is to help change the way you think about money, interest being no different. By becoming the lender you switch to the opposing side which allows you to put money in your wallet, by remaining to be the borrower you continue to take money out of your wallet. The choice is ultimately yours.

Self-Reflection

1. You're young and still have your whole life ahead of you. What type of loans do you plan on using and for what expenses?

2. What future expenses can you use cash for to bypass taking out a loan?

3. What is your perspective on the huge amounts of debt individuals have in America today? How can you be different and escape the debt trap that seems almost inevitable?

PAYING UNCLE SAM

"BACK IN THE YEAR 1789, BENJAMIN FRANKLIN, ONE OF THE FOUNDING FATHERS OF THE UNITED STATES OF AMERICA, ONCE SAID THERE ARE ONLY TWO THINGS CERTAIN IN LIFE…DEATH AND TAXES."

Way back in the year 1789 Benjamin Franklin, one of the founding fathers of the United States of America, once said there are only two things certain in life…" Death and Taxes." Fast forward to the present day and these wise words still hold true with complete certainty. Whenever we get paid by our employer, Uncle Sam makes sure to be there to take his cut. Whenever we go to the market to buy groceries for the week, Uncle Sam makes sure to get his cut. Whenever our car breaks down and needs servicing at a mechanic shop, Uncle Sam is there again to take his cut. Every time there is a recorded monetary transaction, getting paid or making a purchase, Uncle Sam (also known as the United States government) seems to be there to claim his portion of the transaction.

Giving someone else a cut of your hard-earned paycheck every two weeks, and paying that same person a percentage of the transactions you make each and every day may seem and be unfair, but it's required by law to pay taxes and to pay them on time. We can hate it, we can try and fight it, and even try to avoid it all together, but at the end of the day what would benefit us the most is to understand how taxes work to maximize our earning potential in the long term. Before we discuss some of the basic tax terms, we should all be familiar with, let's briefly go over some of the things the government uses our tax money for. The money we pay in taxes is used for a variety of different expenses, but most of it goes to the following:

1. Medicare & Health Programs- helps provide insurance and health coverage for the elderly, disabled, or individuals with specific illnesses.

2. Social Security- a government system that provides monetary assistance to individuals with little to no income. Also, can provide

benefits to individuals who are retired, unemployed, or disabled.

3. Military & Defense- money needed to fund our army, navy, air force, and marines which protect us from external threats.

4. Income Security- a separate program from social security that also provides monetary assistance to individuals who are low income, blind, or disabled. Recipients are required to meet strict income and resource limits.

Definition & Examples

Gross Income: Your total income before having to account for deductions and taxes.

Example 1.

Amanda works forty hours a week and makes $15 dollars per hour. How much does she make per paycheck, per month, and per year?

$15 (dollars per hour) x 40 (works hours per week) = $600 (per week)

Amanda has a gross income of $600 dollars per week.

$600 (per week) x 2 (two weeks) = $1,200 (per paycheck)

Amanda makes a total gross income of $1,200 dollars per paycheck.

$1,200 (per paycheck) x 2 (paychecks per month) = $2,400 (per month)

Amanda makes a total gross income of $2,400 dollars per month,

$2,400 (per month) x 12 (months per year) = $28,800 (per year)

Amanda makes a total gross income of $28,800 dollars per year.

Net Income: your take-home pay after accounting for deductions and withholdings.

Example 2.

Amanda makes a total gross income of $1,200 dollars per paycheck. After accounting for all deductions (Medicare, Social Security, 401k, Health Benefits, etc.) her actual take home pay or net income is $800 dollars.

$800 (per paycheck) x 2 (paychecks per month) = $1,600 (per month)

Amanda has a net income of $1,600 per month.

$1,600 (per month) x 12 (months per year) = $19,200 (per year)

Amanda has a total net income (or take-home pay) of $19,200 dollars per year.

Standard Deduction: a fixed dollar amount that reduces the amount of income you are taxed on. In 2018 the standard deduction for filing single or married filing separately was $12,000, for filing as head of household was $18,000, and for filing as married jointly or qualified widow was $24,000.

Itemized Deduction: a set of individual deductions that together can help lower the amount of income you have to pay taxes on.

Example 3.

Amanda sets up a meeting with her tax professional Lilian to discuss and file her taxes for the year 2018. In order to lower her taxable income, they discuss the pros and cons for the options of the standard deduction vs itemized deductions, with the ultimate goal of choosing the option that will offer the biggest benefit for Amanda. Taking the standard deduction would be easier, more convenient, and would save time. On the other hand, there are hundreds of possible itemized deductions including: medical expenses, property taxes, charitable contributions, and mortgage interest (being the most common). After going over the numbers, Amanda and Lillian decide to file for the standard deduction since Amanda does not have many itemized deductions that she would be able to claim. The standard deduction would offer a bigger refund at this point in time, though that could change in the near or distant future as Amanda's financial situation may change.

Tax laws can be confusing, are constantly changing, and require a lot of time and effort to get a firm understanding of so working with a knowledgeable tax professional whom you trust is very important. Luckily, thanks in much part to advancements and improvements in technology, tax professionals no longer have the obligation to write everything out by hand and can instead plug in numbers in a computer program that tells customers which deductions and options would offer the biggest tax returns. In Amanda's case, she currently does not qualify for many itemized deductions and so the standard deduction offered the biggest benefit. If Amanda did qualify for itemized deductions, perhaps if she was a homeowner and donated money to several charities, it's very likely that opting to take the itemized deductions would offer a bigger refund. It becomes more time consuming as Amanda would also have to provide proof and documentation for those itemized deductions, but because it would lower her tax liability as opposed to the standard deduction it would surely be worth it.

Again, the amount of taxes an individual pays depends on a lot of factors, one of which is the amount of money you make. As you make more and more income as an employee, you will without a doubt notice your gross income increase but also your paycheck taxes and deductions increase along with it. This happens automatically, it's taken from your paycheck before it hits your checking account via direct deposit. There isn't too much you can do about these taxes and deductions unless you have dependents (individuals dependent on your income like kids and a stay-at-home wife) whom you can claim that will allow you to take more of your money home (increase your net income). As a business owner, entrepreneur, or investor, however, you would surely be eligible for more deductions (since you will have more expenses), as well as have access to a much higher income potential. It all depends on the type of investments you make, your profits, your losses, expenses, assets, liabilities, and a wide range of other factors that can collectively give you more access to tax benefits you otherwise wouldn't have access to as an employee.

Money Myths
"Tax time is the best time of the year because I get money back."
-Individuals who have a high income or who make a lot of money also have to pay a large sum of taxes when tax time comes around. They typically do not get refunds and therefore don't necessarily look forward to tax time. On the other hand, individuals who have a low income or who don't make a lot of money typically get tax money back when tax time comes around and do look forward to this time of year. How much we have to pay back or how much

we get back is based on several factors (dependents, deductions, business profits or losses, etc.), but at the end of the day which would you choose…To have a high income? Or to have a low income?

"Everyone has to pay taxes, there's no way around it and worrying about it is just pointless."
-It's true everyone has to pay taxes, but by educating yourself and working with a tax professional you can minimize as much as possible how much you'll have to pay in taxes. By simply not worrying about it or ignoring it all together, you can potentially be throwing money right out the window and miss out on opportunities to lower your tax liability.

Self-Reflection

1. What has been your experience with taxes? When overhearing conversations about paying taxes and getting tax refunds, what types of things are said?

2. Why do you believe people have different perspectives about taxes? How do you believe those perspectives change over time?

3. How will you limit your tax liability? How will you use the tax laws to your advantage to increase the amount of money that flows into your wallet?

Phase Two: Financial Stability

Individuals in the phase of financial stability:

☐   Are in control of their finances.

☐   Can pay for expenses with cash instead of debt.

☐   Regularly contribute to their retirement savings.

☐   Have a sufficient amount of money at their disposal in case of a financial emergency.

☐   Are confident and optimistic about their financial future.

DIFFERENTIATING BETWEEN INCOME & EXPENSES

"IF YOU DON'T FOCUS ON UNDERSTANDING HOW MONEY FLOWS IN AND OUT OF YOUR HANDS YOU WILL BE ON A PATH HEADED STRAIGHT FOR FINANCIAL DISASTER."

This may sound almost elementary, but getting a fundamental understanding of how your money comes in and out of your hands is monumental when it comes to being financially successful. It's astounding today to notice how many people lack insight, don't pay attention, are just plain lazy, or simply don't care to notice how they spend their money and on what they're spending their money on. For purposes of clarity, what we mean when saying money coming in, we're referring to "income" which for 90% percent of Americans comes in the form of employment (having a job). And on the other hand, what we mean when by saying money goes out we're referring to "expenses" which includes bills such as rent, cell phones, and car payments.

Along with understating assets and liabilities (which you will learn about in a later section) your income and expenses are immensely important in understanding your own personal balance sheet. By getting a firm grip on your own balance sheet, you will start to notice the trajectory that you are currently on. If you put the time and effort into reaching your financial goals you will see yourself climbing on an upward trajectory on the road to financial freedom, and if you decide not to focus on understanding how money flows in and out of your hands you will be on a clear downward trajectory headed straight for financial disaster. Believe me, you don't want to be 63 years old and realize you don't have enough money to retire, be faced with a medical emergency you can't pay for or be unable to take your kids on the family vacations you always dreamed of taking them on. It's a sad and painful truth many must face only to realize it's too late to do anything about it.

Definitions & Examples
Income: the monetary payment received for goods and services, or from other sources, such as rents or investments.

Example1.

Laura works as a Cashier at CVS and makes $12 per hour. She works thirty hours per week which equates to $360 per week:

$12 (dollars per hour) x 30 (hours per week) = $360 (dollars per week)

She gets paid every two weeks which equals $720.

$360 (dollars per week) x 2 (two weeks) = $720 (every two weeks)

But that's before she pays taxes and deductions. After taxes and deductions, she takes home about $550 every two weeks. Which means that every month she takes home about $1,100.

$550 (take home pay every two weeks) x 2 (two paychecks per month) = $1,100 (take home pay per month)

Not too shabby.

Expenses: a cost or a charge for goods or services. Money spent on something.

Example 2.

Laura lives with her parents and helps pay for a portion of the rent. At the moment, she has a room to herself and pays $300 per month. She also has a brand-new iPhone and pays for her share of the phone service on the family plan, which on average is about $150 per month. Furthermore, Laura is still making payments on her 2020 Toyota Corolla which with insurance comes out to about $400 per month. Every now and again, Laura also enjoys browsing for deals on Amazon, she has a Prime account and gets super-fast delivery, on average she spends about $100 per month. If we add all of her expenses up, what will we see?

$300 (rent) + $150 (iPhone bill) + $400 (car payment & insurance) + $100 (amazon shopping) = $950 (total expenses)

If we were to extract Laura's monthly expenses from her monthly take-home pay how much would we have left over?

$1,100 (take home pay) – $950 (monthly expenses) = $150 (cash left over at the end of the month)

At the end of every month, Laura on average has a grand total of $150 cash left over. What we haven't mentioned yet is that Laura also pays for gas, groceries, lunch (at work), and going out with friends (leisure), but instead of using cash she puts it all on her credit card which has a $1,000 credit limit. Her credit card is nearly maxed out ($920), and she continues to make minimum monthly payments of just $25 dollars per month.

Now, if you had to take a wild guess, is Laura on a path to becoming financially free? Is she on an upward financial trajectory, or on a downward financial trajectory? Do you think she's paying attention to how much money she's taking home and how much money she's spending? From the details given about Laura's financial situation and spending habits alone, we can easily conclude that she's presently not on a path to financial freedom and accumulating long-term wealth. Laura may believe that she's saving $150 per month because that's how much "cash" she has left over every month, but because she uses her credit card to finance other expenditures of her life, she in actuality isn't saving any money at all!

And we haven't even considered how much using her credit card is actually costing her (in interest payments alone). So not only is she on a clear downward trajectory, but she is also underwater and sinking lower and lower each and every month the more she spends, also known as "drowning in debt."

This is all too common in society today. Without paying attention to how income ties into expenses, many individuals are setting themselves up for financial disaster without even realizing it. On the flip side, individuals who take the time to track their income, track their expenses, see the relationship between the two, and make adjustments so that at the end of the month they are actually able to save and/or invest money as opposed to drowning in debt are the ones who win in the game of money and get ahead. By no means is this difficult but does require a conscious effort.

Money Myths
"There is too much month at the end of the Money."
- For many individuals this is unfortunately true. They simply have too many expenses at the end of the month and don't have enough money to cover those expenses. This results in constantly having to borrow more and more money to cover those expenses.

"Tracking Income and Expenses is too much Work."
- Tracking your income and expenses takes work, yes. But it doesn't require a lot of work at all. You can

easily set up an excel spreadsheet, set up two separate tables or columns, label one "income" and the other "expenses", and simply fill in all your sources of income and all your expenses during the month. From there, you can go back in and make adjustments whether your income or expenses increase or decrease, and you can easily see how much money is coming in and how much money is going back out.

Self-Reflection

1. In order to have more income at the end of the month, what expenses can you cut and live without?

2. Are all expenses bad? Explain.

3. How will you keep track of where your income goes and what your expenses are? Are there applications or programs you can use to make the tracking of your money easy?

LEARNING HOW TO BUDGET

"HOW USEFUL IS LEARNING HOW TO MAKE A LOT OF MONEY IF YOU NEVER LEARN HOW TO KEEP IT?"

Being able to budget your money and actually being able to stick to that budget is just as important, if not more important, as learning how to make a lot of money. After all, how useful is learning how to make a lot of money if you never learn how to keep it? For many of us, learning how to budget requires a combination of discipline, hard work, communication, impulse control, emotional intelligence, and the ability to resist temptation (just to name a few). These skills and traits can be very difficult to attain especially when we consider how in this day and age online shopping is so prominent making it incredibly easy for us to make a purchase. A purchase can literally take place at the click of a button! But budgeting is something that must be done in order to achieve our financial goals.

Definitions & Examples

Budget: an estimate of expected income and expenses for a given period of time in the future.

Example 1.

David is planning on attending Valley College in the fall and has been working at Wal-Mart as a part-time sales associate to save money to pay for his first semester. He currently makes $12 an hour and has been able to save up $800 in total for his upcoming college expenses. For this first semester he plans on taking 5 classes, each costing around $150. With processing fees, parking expenses, and books, he's looking at a grand total of approximately $1300.

$150 x 5 (classes) = $750 (total for classes)

$300 (parking) + $165 (books) + $85 (processing fees) = $550 (total for enrollment fees)

$750 (total for classes) + $550 (total for enrollment fees) = $1300 (grand total)

How much more does David need to save up to have enough cash to pay for his first semester of college?

$1300 (total college tuition) − $800 (total David has in savings) = $500 (David needs)

David still needs $500 dollars to have enough money to pay for his first semester of college. David has one month left to save and if all goes according to plan, he should be able to save up the extra five hundred dollars he needs for his first semester. A group of his close friends, however, are planning a weekend getaway, and have been urging David to come along. They are planning for the weekend right before David is to start college and tell him that by splitting all the expenses (gas, food, hotel room, drinks) they believe they will spend $200 or less. David doesn't want to miss out on all the fun and decides to go.

He leaves with $250, goes, has a great time, and comes back home owing his buddy $50. He doesn't have enough money to pay for school, so he'll need to ask his parents to loan him some money or get his first credit card and charge the remaining school expenses on that credit card.

In the example given, by no means are we implying that budgeting and "fun" are polar opposites. And by no means are we saying you shouldn't go out and have fun. In fact, going out and having fun while you're young and don't have the responsibilities of raising a family is absolutely something you should do. Not only will it allow you to not have regrets when you're older, but traveling and sharing experiences with people you love and care about is a wonderful thing that can help you develop into a better person.

However, in this specific scenario (keep in mind that everyone's situation is different), David had his mind set on prioritizing payment for his college tuition expenses but wasn't able to accomplish his goal because he made the choice to prioritize having fun with his friends instead. Not only that, but he went over his budget and will have to finance the extra money he now needs to pay for college. And because this is his first experience setting a financial goal, he's negatively reinforcing the idea that prioritizing partying while financing other expenses is okay. Which can become a big problem, by mounting debt on top of more debt, if it becomes a habit.

Money Myths
"Budgeting is for broke people."
- Budgeting should be exercised by everyone, whether rich or poor. Believe it or not, affluent families and individuals are much more likely to budget than families and individuals who experience financial distress. Affluent families and individuals usually have

a certain amount of money they allocate for fun, another certain amount of money allocated for living expenses, a certain amount of money allocated for saving, and certain amount allocated for investing. Individuals and families who experience financial distress on the other hand tend to have enough to pay for some of their living expenses and choose to finance (use loans and credit cards) to pay for luxuries such as a nice home, having nice furniture, taking vacations, and buying nice cars.

"I can't enjoy life to the fullest by budgeting."
- It is 100% possible to enjoy living life to the fullest while also staying within a budget. If you're unable to budget and enjoy life simultaneously you are more likely to have an income problem than a budgeting problem. In other words, you're not making enough money to afford the lifestyle you desire or imagine yourself having.

"Budgeting requires too much math, and I was never good at math."
- Budgeting does require math, but nothing more complicated than simple addition and subtraction. You

can go to a first-grade classroom and meet small children that are more than capable of solving equations involving addition and subtraction. Someone saying they can't budget because they're not good at math is making excuses and lacks the motivation to budget.

Self-Reflection

1. How have your experiences with budgeting money turned out on previous occasions?

2. What issues can you anticipate ahead of time when attempting to set a budget for yourself and sticking to that budget?

3. Have you ever bought something on impulse, and then regretted that decision afterward? How can you prevent buying on impulse in the future?

CHOOSING BETWEEN LEASING & OWNING

"SHOULD I BUY A HOME, OR RENT AN APARTMENT? SHOULD I BUY A CAR OR LEASE A CAR?"

Some of the most highly debated questions amongst young adults today involve…. Should I buy a home, or rent an apartment? Should I buy a car or lease a car? Well, if you were to ask someone who is of an older generation the answer is clear: Buying is always better than renting! It's better to own your house or car rather than rent because renting is simply a way to throw your money away. And on the surface that may seem to be true. When you buy something, it becomes yours (in theory), and when you rent something, you're simply borrowing it. At the end of the day, you'd like to get something in return for your money…right? But is that all there really is to this argument? The answer is No.

The issue with the older generation's mindset is that they became young adults in the 1970s, 1980s, and 1990s, and back then real estate, cars, and other items were relatively cheaper. In addition, there were overall less people in the general population and therefore less competition, and the value of the dollar was much higher than it is today. It made more sense for them to opt to buy when they were young, the economy was strong and on a clear upwards trajectory. And for those that did choose to buy will tell you endlessly… "I bought my house for $200,000 dollars twenty years ago and now it's worth $620,000! It's the best investment I ever made!" (you'll rarely hear a statement like this about a car).

But as you will quickly find out in later sections of this book, there are a lot of hidden costs they fail to tell you about, which complicates the argument just a bit. By no means is it a simple linear equation:

$620,000 (home value today) - $200,000 (purchase price twenty years ago) = $420,000 (total profit)

Although the older person who bought a house twenty years ago for two hundred thousand dollars still owns the same house that is now worth six hundred thousand dollars believes he or she has made a profit of four hundred and twenty thousand dollars, that is inaccurate to say the least.

Definitions & Examples

Leasing/Renting: having temporary ownership of an item with restrictions on what you can do with it.

Example 1.

When you rent or lease an apartment, you'll likely be required to put down a certain amount of money as a security deposit, and the contract of agreement will generally be for at least a year (in some cases can be month to month) where you'll be required to make a payment toward the rent at the beginning of every month to the owner.

Example 2.

When you rent or lease a car, you'll likely be required to put money down as a down payment (though not always), and the contract will usually be for 1-3 years requiring you to make monthly payments to the company that owns the car. You may also have a mileage restriction on the car (usually 12,000-15,000 miles per year). If you go over the mileage limit, you'll likely have to pay a fee.

Ownership: having the right of possession.

Example 3.

When you buy a home, you'll be required to put money down for the down payment, pay for closing costs, pay for property taxes every year, pay for homeowners insurance, pay for private mortgage insurance if your down payment is less than 20% percent, and make a payment toward your mortgage every month (principal and interest).

Example 4.

When you buy a car you'll be required to put money down for a down payment, pay documentation and processing fees, pay for title and registration fees, pay for GAP (Guaranteed Auto Protection) insurance if you choose to get it, pay for any upgrades to the car (window tint, rims, etc.), and make monthly car payments to the company that financed your purchase (principal and interest).

As I mentioned before, figuring out whether the best decision for you would be to buy or lease is somewhat complicated. When assessing the true cost of an item it's important to consider what the price is, how much value the item will deliver for you, and how much time you'll be able to save by having the item. Most individuals assess whether to make a purchase or not based on price alone, which again is important, but not sufficient. Let's consider further buying and leasing a new car.

When it comes to buying or leasing a car, if we compared the pros and cons in the short term when it came to price, value, and time the likely best decision to make would be to lease. How so? When it comes to price, leasing a car is cheaper because you don't necessarily have to put money down for a down payment. And this impacts value because you're able to retain cash in your savings account that you can then utilize to fund the purchase of assets, put money into your business, or purchase other investments. This will also save you time because you'll be leasing a relatively new car which will still be covered by manufacturer's warranty and maintenance/repairs are sometimes included in the lease agreement, meaning you won't have to spend time or money at a car shop waiting for your car to get fixed after breaking down. So again, when considering the short term (1-3 years), by leasing you'll be able to drive a new car, have a lower monthly payment, keep more of your cash, and not have to worry about repairs.

By looking at the long term however (5-15 years), the better decision might very well be to opt to buy a car. Not necessarily a new car, but a used/reliable car. When purchasing a certified pre-owned vehicle, you'll usually be able to buy at a discount (because the car is used), and because you're buying at a lower price your monthly payments and the depreciation on the vehicle over time will be less. Also, after five years you will likely have been able to pay off your car (principal and interest), meaning you'll own your car free and clear without having to make more monthly payments to the company that financed your purchase. Though, at the end of five or ten years you'll have a much older car (especially since you bought it used) that may constantly give you problems and need repairing, possibly leading you to buy a newer vehicle. Buying a brand-new car right from the start will flat out cost you more overtime and will be subject to higher rates of depreciation. In fact, it has been determined that on average your brand-new car will lose 20% of its value over the first twelve months, and then over the next four years will continue to lose 10% of its value!

Money Myths

"When considering buying versus leasing it's really a matter of what offers me the lower monthly payment."

- As we've discussed, monthly payment is only one of many factors you need to consider when making the decision to buy or lease. It's a matter of what your goals are, and depending on what your goals are will determine what you value most when making your final decision.

"Rent is super high in many areas across the U.S., it's cheaper to buy a home."

- Rent is definitely high in many areas and will continue to rise, however home prices will only continue to rise right along with them. Can your monthly payment really be cheaper if you buy instead of rent? Yes, it can. Though, in order to make that happen you'll need to put a significant amount of cash down in order to get your monthly payment to a level where it's lower than the rental rates in the surrounding areas. So, in the end would it actually be cheaper?

Self-Reflection

1. What role does having cash on hand play in the decision to buy or lease?

2. Think about your future self. Do you anticipate periods in your life where it will make more sense to buy a home instead of rent an apartment? And vice versa, do you anticipate periods in your life where it will make more sense to rent an apartment instead of buying a home?

3. Again, think about your future self. Do you anticipate periods in your life where it will make more sense to buy a car instead of lease? And vice versa, do you anticipate periods in your life where it will make more sense to lease a car instead of buying a car?

INVESTING IN BONDS

"BY INVESTING IN A BOND, YOU BECOME THE ONE LOANING MONEY TO THE FEDERAL GOVERNMENT AND THE FEDERAL GOVERNMENT IN RETURN PAYS YOU INTEREST FOR HAVING LOANED THEM THAT MONEY."

In the very same way that consumers use debt to finance purchases, there are times where the government as well as corporate entities also use debt to finance a purchase they need to keep up with their operating expenses. How do the government and corporations raise the capital they need? By issuing bonds that investors can then purchase and earn a return on. It's essentially the same concept as taking out a school loan to go to college. The federal government usually loans students a certain amount of money and charges interest for that loan. But in bonds the tables turn. By investing in a bond, you now become the one loaning money to the federal government and the federal government in return pays you interest for having loaned them that money. Pretty cool right?

Furthermore, bonds are considered to be a "much safer" type of investment than say the stock market which we'll talk more about in a later section. Bonds are considered to be a safer investment for a few different reasons.

1. Prices don't fluctuate on a day-to-day basis in the same way stock prices do.
2. The risk of losing your investment is smaller when investing in bonds than it is when investing in stocks.
3. Bonds pay investors a fixed amount of interest that is backed by a promise from the issuer. Meanwhile, some stocks pay dividends, but the issuer does not have an obligation to make these payments to shareholders.

With that being said it's important to keep in mind that bonds are a different type of investment in comparison to stocks and real estate. It's up to the person investing their hard-earned money to do the research and determine whether or not bonds have a place in their investment portfolio.

Definitions & Examples

Bond: a fixed income investment that represents a loan made to a corporate entity or the government.

Coupon Rate: the interest rate earned by the bondholder in return for lending money to the borrower.

Example 1.

Frank is a young 20-year-old college student who has been working two jobs to put himself through college. He's doing well for himself and has been able to accumulate $7,000 in savings thus far. Frank doesn't have any debt, isn't planning to have any big expenses in the near future and begins to wonder what he can do to help his money grow instead of just having it sit in his bank account. He does some research and is fascinated by the idea of purchasing a government bond. He finds out that historically government bonds are very safe to invest in, will pay interest twice a year, and can be held long-term or sold above face value if the opportunity presents itself.

Frank goes online and purchases a two-thousand-dollar 5 year bond with a 2.75% coupon rate. If Frank decides to hold this bond for the entire five years, this is how much money in interest he can expect to make:

$2,000 (purchase price) x 0.0275 (interest rate) = $55 per year

Frank will make fifty-five dollars per year, and since this bond pays investors twice a year that means Frank will be paid

$55 (per year) / 2 (twice per year) = $27.50 (every six months)

Frank will be paid twenty-seven dollars and fifty cents every six months. Now, over the course of five years:

$55 (per year) x 5 (five years) = $275 (total interest paid)

Frank can expect to make two hundred and seventy-five dollars in total interest after five years, and once the bond reaches maturity (five year agreement), Frank will also be paid back his original investment of two thousand dollars.

Some of you might be thinking… Why the heck would I tie up two thousand dollars for five years to make a measly two hundred and seventy-five bucks? It doesn't seem like a whole lot of money, does it? But we must be reminded of a few things. One, bonds are considered to be a much safer form of investing, which usually also means a lower rate of return. On the flip side, when investments offer a much higher rate of return it usually also comes with added risk. Two, we must consider the amount of money that is to be invested. If Frank had the ability to instead invest five thousand, ten thousand, or fifty thousand dollars into a government bond, the amount of interest he would earn back would also increase. Three, when it comes to investing money, we must also think about creating a diversified portfolio. That's just a fancy way of saying you should have a balanced mix of investments, some low risk, some medium risk, and some high-risk investments. Again, bonds would be considered to be at the lower end of the spectrum, being lower risk investments in comparison to other investment options.

All in all, bonds are an excellent way to get started in investing. Will investing in bonds make you rich fast? No. Will you make a ton of money? Probably not. Bonds don't have the same appeal that say cannabis stocks or cryptocurrencies do promising to make you rich overnight, but because they are safe and backed by a promise from the issuer it nearly guarantees you will make a return on your money.

And when comparing investing in bonds versus having money sit in a savings account accumulating an incredibly small amount of interest, most banks will pay 0.01%, bonds are clearly the better option.

Money Myths
"Bonds are investments for old people."
-Young or old bond investments should have a place in everyone's portfolio. Bonds do tend to be favored by older individuals getting ready to retire for the simple reason that their goal is usually to preserve their wealth instead of engaging in high-risk investments that will put their retirement income in a very vulnerable place. Whereas younger individuals have time on their side and can afford to take higher risks with their money. Though investment balance and diversification should be exercised.

"You can't buy Bonds at a discount."
-It actually is possible to purchase bonds below value, which allows investors to have the potential to sell bonds before their maturity date for a profit. Cutting fees from brokers and middlemen and instead buying

bonds direct can increase your potential to earn a profit.

Self-Reflection

1. Are bonds a part of your long-term investment plan? Why or why not?

2. Go online and research the basic differences between different types of bonds. What types of bonds seem to be the more appealing investment choice? What makes these bonds more appealing than the others?

CONTRIBUTING TO YOUR 401K

"THE VAST MAJORITY OF INDIVIDUALS DON'T HAVE THE SLIGHTEST CLUE AS TO HOW MUCH MONEY THEY ACTUALLY NEED TO SAVE IN ORDER TO RETIRE AND MAINTAIN A GOOD QUALITY OF LIFE."

Being able to retire comfortably without worry is a goal most individuals have as they get closer and closer to retirement age, and understandably so. After all, who wants to be nearing retirement age and find out they don't have nearly enough money saved in their retirement accounts to at least pay for the basics of life necessities let alone pay for luxuries such as vacation and travel? It's a scary thought, and unfortunately the vast majority of people don't have even the slightest clue as to how much money they actually need to save in order to retire and maintain a good quality of life. Nonetheless, 401k plans are excellent and a key component to retirement income that we should all take advantage of. Anyone who works for a company that offers a 401k plan, some companies do, and some companies don't, should begin putting money into their 401k as quickly as possible.

What makes a 401k such a good investment? Or maybe even a better question, what are people missing out on by not investing in a 401k? Individuals who don't invest in a 401k miss out on a few benefits, but here are the top four:

1. Automatic savings deductions
2. Free money with an employer match
3. Tax breaks
4. Compound interest

We'll talk more about these benefits in our economic blueprint section, but for now let's define what a 401k is and go over some examples that you'll likely encounter as you begin your journey in the job market.

Definition & Examples
401k: a retirement savings plan that is sponsored by your employer. This plan allows employees to save and invest a part of their paycheck before taxes are taken out.

Example 1.

Beatrice is a new hire at Johnson & Johnson and is working in the field as a Business Account Representative. She's been working for nearly two months and is making approximately $45,000 dollars per year. As soon as she started her job, she made the decision to sign up for the employer matched 401k plan in order to take advantage of all the benefits. Every two weeks she makes approximately:

$45,000 (dollars per year) / 12 (twelve months) = $3,750 (dollars per month)

$3,750 (dollars per month) / 2 (paid every two weeks) = $1,875 (every two weeks)

Beatrice earns one thousand eight hundred and seventy-five dollars every two weeks in gross income (before taxes and deductions). Her 401k investment plan currently deducts 6% of her paycheck every two weeks, which means:

$1,875 (every two weeks) x 0.06 (401k deduction) = $112.5 (deduction every two weeks)

Her 401k deducts one hundred and twelve dollars and fifty cents every two weeks from her paycheck.

Vested: refers to the ownership of your 401k and determines how much of your 401k funds you can take with you when you leave the company.

Example 2.

Johnson & Johnson requires their employees to be employed at their company for five years in order to be fully vested in the company. Therefore, if Beatrice wants to receive her full 401k compensation benefits, she will need to be employed by Johnson & Johnson for at least five years. If she decides to quit her job and leave the company after three years, she would receive all the money she has contributed to her 401k but only a portion of what the company has matched to her plan.

0 to 1 years of employment, 0% vested

1 to 2 years of employment, 20% vested

2 to 3 years of employment, 40% vested

3 to 4 years of employment, 60% vested

4 to 5 years of employment, 80% vested

5 years or more of employment, 100% vested

After three years of employment Beatrice would only receive sixty percent of her 401k employer matched benefits. In a sense, she'd be leaving free money on the table.

Contribution Limit: the Internal Revenue Service (IRS) has adjusted the 401k contribution limit to be $19,000 per year for employees, as of 2019.
Example 3.

If Beatrice worked at Johnson & Johnson for 10, 20, or 30 years, and continuously received promotions working her way up the corporate ladder, it would be wise for her to also continuously increase her 401k contributions. Because again, it's like getting free money from your employer. There is a limit, however set by the IRS to how much employees can contribute to their plan. This amount generally increases (slightly) every year, as of 2019 the maximum amount Beatrice would be able to contribute to her 401k is $19,000.

Consistently and continuously contributing to a 401k retirement plan, especially early on in our working career can pay a huge amount of dividends later on. Let's revisit the benefits we mentioned in our introduction to this topic:

1. Automatic savings deductions
- 401k plans make it incredibly easy for you to save money by automating the entire process.

Contributions are automatically deducted from your paycheck, which means you don't have to actively or consciously manage your money (which can sometimes be a pain in the butt).

2. Free money with an employer match

- Most companies will match a certain portion of contributions to your 401k. This is essentially free money that you should maximize and take advantage of.

3. Tax breaks

- When contributing to a 401k you can take advantage of two major tax breaks. One, your contributions take place when you get paid but are taken before deductions, meaning you get to invest with pre-tax dollars (not after-tax dollars). Two, the more you invest in a 401k the more it lowers your taxable income at the end of the year. Cushioning the amount of taxes you'll have to pay.

4. Compound interest

- As you continuously contribute to your 401k plan you continue to earn interest on the money that has been earning interest over time.

Even after seeing the great benefits 401k plans offer, if you're still thinking to yourself "The money I work hard for is mine and should be going directly to my bank account," you're right. It's hard seeing your paycheck dwindle down from total gross income, having to pay taxes, having to pay for health benefits, and then on top of that funding a 401k. By the time you get your net income, your take home pay, your paycheck can literally seem like it's been cut in half! Which can be very difficult to look at let alone be enough money to live off of. But this in essence is one of the fundamental concepts in accumulating wealth…living below your means and prioritizing saving and investing.

By not investing in a 401k, you may risk having more of your money be eaten by taxes when tax time comes around, and if you're not good at managing your money you'd likely spend the extra income on luxuries rather than income producing assets anyway. Which again is a choice you have every right to make, but if your goal is to accumulate wealth you absolutely must make sound financial decisions over extended periods of time. Not all 401k plans are created equal so it's important to do your research and ask about your benefits when accepting a new job. All in all, 401k plans can be an excellent investment vehicle that'll help you retire comfortably when your time to retire finally arrives.

Money Myths
"My 401k account should be sufficient enough for me to retire."
-Individuals who earned a high income throughout their working careers and maximized their 401k contributions may have enough to retire solely on their 401k, but this isn't the case for most middle-class Americans earning an average salary. Most individuals will need a multitude of funds to have enough to retire comfortably.

"It's not worth it to be employed at a company long enough to be vested if you can earn a higher salary elsewhere."
-This can be tricky. It may seem that leaving for a higher paying job is always the better option, but that isn't always the case. Again, some companies offer great retirement benefits and some not so great. If you are earning a decent salary, regularly contributing

to a 401k plan with a company that offers a generous match, and leave for another job paying a higher salary, but the company offers a mediocre match you might be making a mistake. You must also consider how vested you are in your current plan, if you leave before being fully vested you'd be leaving money on the table. Then again, if you have a plan for the money you'll be earning with a higher salary like say funding your side business, then your earning potential in the long term may increase. There are multiple considerations you must take into account in order to make a good decision.

Self-Reflection

1. Ask your parents, teachers, or guardians about 401k retirement plans. Do they have one? Do they regularly contribute? Why or why not?

2. How do you plan on taking advantage of a 401k? If you are currently employed, are you regularly contributing? Why or why not?

3. Do some online research. What are some common mistakes people make when investing

in their 401k? What penalties are involved when cashing out their 401k early?

Phase Three: Financial Security

Individuals in the phase of financial security:

☐ Utilize debt to generate more income, not to finance their lifestyle.

☐ Consistently increase their net worth by buying assets, investing, and saving.

☐ Aren't worried about losing their job. They have multiple streams of income they can rely on to pay for their expenses.

☐ Have complete confidence they can retire comfortably.

UNDERSTANDING INFLATION

"I REMEMBER WHEN I WAS A KID GAS WAS $0.69 CENTS A GALLON AND WE COULD FILL UP A TANK OF GAS WITH JUST TEN BUCKS"

The concept of inflation is something most of us have heard about in some sense, but usually is never explained to us in detail and therefore most of us don't understand the implications it can have and does have on our long-term financial objectives. Let's consider an example.... think back to a time when you were a child, riding in the backseat of a car on a long road trip with your parents beginning to run low on gas so mom or dad decide to pull over to the gas station and fill up. They look at the prices and say "Wow $3.89 per gallon?! I remember when I was a kid gas was $0.69 cents a gallon and my dad could fill up a tank of gas with just ten bucks!" When it comes to our generation it's hard to imagine being able to pay sixty-nine cents per gallon on gas and being able to fill up a tank of gas for only $10 dollars. And we might feel that our parents are exaggerating just a tad because sometimes they randomly do, but when it comes to telling us about these hard to believe low prices, they're usually telling us the truth.

The fact of the matter is items are much more expensive now than they were back then. And whether we like it or not, prices will continue to rise each and every year. This is consistent with the concept of inflation which in short measures the increase in prices on a year-by-year basis and accounts for the loss of purchasing power when it comes to your money. That's right, your money loses value each and every year! On average, your money loses approximately three percent of its value every year. At first glance three percent may not seem like a lot, but over time it begins to add up fairly quickly. Millions of individuals don't understand inflation and is yet another reason why so many struggle financially and aren't able to get ahead throughout their lifetime.

Definitions & Examples
Inflation: a general increase in prices and fall in the purchasing value of money.
Example 1.

If you were to set aside $100 from your paycheck and hide them under your mattress, left that money there for an entire year, and pulled them out to use for a purchase.... your actual buying power would be less (roughly $97) than it was the year before when you initially set that money aside. Furthermore, if you were to keep that same hundred dollars under the mattress for a second year, those same hundred dollars would then be worth roughly $94. And if you kept that same hundred dollars under your mattress for a third year, your money would then be worth about $91. In other words, if your money isn't growing it's actually losing value the longer it sits there.

Many of you might say... "This doesn't apply to me or anyone in the present day. No one hides their money under a mattress anymore, everyone deposits their money into a bank account." Which is true. Now and days most of us, if not all of us, put our money in a checking or savings account where our money is safe. Furthermore, most savings accounts will pay you interest for parking your money there. However, the national average when it comes to savings account interest paid is only 0.10%. That means if you had a thousand dollars in your savings account, at the end of the year you would be paid:

$1,000 (money in savings account) x 0.001 (interest per year) = $1 (total interest made)

You would make a staggering one dollar for the year. Let's consider a bigger number. If you had ten thousand dollars in your savings account and had it there for a year you would be paid:

$10,000 (money in savings account) x 0.001(interest per year) = $10 (total interest made)

Your return for having ten thousand dollars with your bank would return you a grand total of ten dollars per year.

So, in reality is your bank savings account really protecting you against inflation? Not at all! You're only making 0.10% percent on your money meanwhile inflation is eating 3% percent of your money as it sits there. Your bank on the other hand is turning around, lending your money to other people through mortgages, loans, and credit cards, and charging people interest on that money anywhere between 4%-24% percent! Your bank is without question staying ahead of inflation and turning a profit.

How can you protect yourself and try to stay ahead of inflation? One of the easiest and safest ways to combat inflation is to open up a savings account with a bank that pays you a higher interest rate. Ally Bank is a good option for this. At the time of writing, Ally Bank pays its customers 4.2% percent interest on their savings accounts. That's 42 times higher than the national average of 0.10%. If we did the same math with having $1,000 dollars and $10,000 in a savings account but now factored in what Ally would pay we would get:

$1,000 (money in savings account) x 0.042 (Ally interest per year) = $42 (total interest made)

$10,000 (money in savings account) x 0.042 (Ally interest per year) = $420 (total interest made)

With a thousand dollars in an Ally bank savings account we would get a return of forty-two dollars per year, and with ten thousand dollars in an Ally bank savings account we would get a return of four hundred and twenty dollars per year. Much better!

An even better option to stay ahead of inflation would be to invest your money, which does involve risk that we will talk about in later sections. Depending on what you invest in (stocks, real estate, crowd funding, certified deposits, bonds, etc.) you will have the ability to earn a higher return on your money. And by having your money work for you while getting a higher return on your money, you'll be able to avoid the trap of having your money sit and lose its buying power with each passing day.

Money Myths
"Saving money is the Key to Retirement."
- Parents everywhere will preach that saving money is the key to retirement, which is false. Saving money is definitely important especially when it comes to having cash on hand for an unexpected emergency, but investing and growing your money is far more important when it comes to retirement. High net worth individuals will agree, while individuals of the middle class will continue to believe saving is their best and safest option.

"Inflation affects everyone and therefore is unavoidable."
- It's true that inflation affects everyone, but it affects some individuals differently than others. And this has to do more with being a consumer versus being an entrepreneur/investor. When you're a consumer, you

buy goods and services at the price that is set. You have an option of what goods and services you may want to buy but have no control over their prices. When you're an entrepreneur however, you are the person that sets the price. You can increase the cost of your goods and services whenever you deem necessary to help improve your bottom line and off-set the cost of inflation. Pretty sweet right?

Self-Reflection

1. How do you plan on progressively staying ahead of inflation and rising costs of living?

2. By failing to invest your money at an early age, how will inflation affect your finances in the future?

3. Think critically. Can inflation ever be a good sign for the overall economy? Why or why not?

DIFFERENTIATING BETWEEN ASSETS & LIABILITIES

"MANY PEOPLE GO THROUGH LIFE WITH VERY LITTLE FINANCIAL EDUCATION AND MAKE THE CRITICAL MISTAKE OF BUYING LIABILITIES THAT THEY BELIEVE ARE ASSETS."

Making the distinction between what assets are and what liabilities are is crucial in understanding your personal financial situation. Many people unfortunately go through life with very little financial education and make the critical mistake of buying liabilities that they believe are assets, instead of buying assets that truly are assets. In doing so, they leave themselves extremely vulnerable and in a very risky position to be left with nothing when financial hardships arise. Whether it comes in the form of losing employment, needing money to pay for medical emergencies, or having to come up with a large sum of cash, banks and financial institutions likely won't loan money if the individual possesses a significant amount of liabilities and not enough cash or assets to off-set those liabilities. Confused? Let's dig in...

Definitions & Examples

Asset: an item of ownership that puts money in your wallet every month.

Liability: an item of ownership that takes money out of your wallet every month.

Example 1.

You save up $20,000 over the course of 5 years. You decide to buy a house for $100,000 in an up-and-coming neighborhood in Phoenix Arizona and rent it out. You spend $20,000 in down payment and closing costs, and take out an $80,000 loan from the bank at 4% interest for 30 yrs.

To get our monthly mortgage (principal and interest) we'll need to do some math.

$80,000 (loan total) / 30 (30-year repayment plan) = $2,666 (yearly principal payment)

Your total yearly principal payment is $2,666.

To get our monthly principal payment we'll need to divide by 12 (months in a year).

$2,666 (yearly principal payment) / 12 (months in a year) = $222 (monthly principal payment)

Your monthly principal payment is $222.

To get our interest payment we'll need to multiply our loan amount and our interest rate.

$80,000 (loan total) x .04 (interest rate) = $3,200 (yearly interest payment)

Your total yearly interest payment is $3,200.

To get our monthly interest payment we'll again have to divide by 12 (months in a year).

$3,200 (yearly interest payment) / 12 (months in a year) = $266 (monthly interest payment)

Your total monthly interest payment is $266.

Now we can combine our monthly principal payment and our monthly interest to get our total mortgage payment.

$222 (monthly principal) + $266 (monthly interest) = $488 (total mortgage payment)

Your total monthly mortgage payment is $488.

Now, if we rent out our house for $750 per month, that means we'd make a positive cashflow of:

$750 (rent to someone else) - $488 (monthly mortgage) = $262, cash in your wallet every month.

Over the course of a year (12 months) that equates to:

$262 (monthly cashflow) x 12 (months in a year) = $3,144, per year in your wallet.

And over the course of 30 years that would equate to $3,144 (yearly cashflow) x 30 (years) = $94,320, cash in your wallet.

And because your loan would be paid off after 30 years (because you were on a 30-year loan repayment plan), that would mean that on the 31st year the entire payment of rent would go straight into your wallet!

(please note that the example above does not account for taxes, insurance, depreciation, appreciation, maintenance, upkeep, and repairs)

Example 2.

You save up $5,000 over the course of 2 years. You decide to buy a brand-new BMW for $30,000, all black with beautiful leather interior. You put a $5,000 down payment and borrow the other $25,000 from the car dealership at 5% interest for 5 years.

To get our monthly car payment (principal and interest) we'll again need to do some math.

$25,000 (total loan) / 5 (five years) = $5,000 (yearly principal payment)

Your yearly principal payment is $5,000.

To get our monthly principal payment we'll need to divide by 12 (months in a year).

$5,000 (yearly principal) / 12 (months in a year) = $416 (monthly principal payment)

Your monthly principal payment will be $416.

To get our interest payment we'll need to multiply our loan amount by our interest rate.

$25,000 (loan total) x .05 (interest rate) = $1,250 (yearly interest payment)

Your total yearly interest payment is $1,250.

To get our monthly interest payment we'll again need to divide by 12 (months in a year).

$1,250 (yearly interest) / 12 (months in a year) = $104 (monthly interest payment)

Your monthly interest payment is $104.

Now we can combine our monthly principal payment and monthly interest payment to get our total monthly car payment.

$416 (monthly principal payment) + $104 (monthly interest payment) = $520 (total monthly car payment)

Your total monthly car payment is $520.

By the time you're finished paying for your car 5 years later how much would the total equate to?

$520 (total monthly payment) x 12 (months in a year) = $6,240 (total payments per year)

$6,240 (payments per year) x 5 (years)= $31,200 (total in 5 years)

Over the course of 5 years, you would pay $31,200. At the end of the day what is your car really costing you?

$31,200 (total payments) + $5,000 (initial down payment) = $36,200.

Including your down payments and total payments over five years your car total would equate to $36,200.

(please note that this example does not account for taxes, insurance, depreciation, maintenance, upkeep, and repairs)

Again, notice how the rental property is putting $262 in cash every month in your wallet, and the car is taking $520 in cash every month out of your wallet. Now, we're not saying buying a BMW is wrong or a bad thing. In fact, if buying a brand-new BMW is one of your goals then you should absolutely do it. The point I'm trying to drive across is that if your ultimate goal is to learn how to make a lot of money then you should opt to buy things that will allow you to do exactly that, make a lot of money. Some people may argue that a car is an asset because without a car they wouldn't be able to go to work, but if we use the simple definitions: assets put money in your wallet every month while liabilities take money out of your wallet every month, then we'll see that a car cannot be classified as an asset (unless you figure out a way for your car to put money in your wallet like leasing it to someone else or driving lyft/uber).

Not to mention that your investment property will appreciate over time (increase in value) while your car will depreciate over time (decrease in value). You might often hear your parents say… "we bought this house back in 2004 for $200,000 and now it's worth $380,000, best investment we've ever made!" Which solely in terms of appreciation is true. Most homes across the entire United States appreciate in value at a rate of around 5% every year. The only time you might hear something like this about a car is when someone buys an old busted up car, fixes it up, and then re-sells it at a higher price (also known as flipping). But that is considered more restoration than it is appreciation over time. It's actually the opposite for a car. We again remind you that on average your brand-new car will lose 20% of its value over the first twelve months, and then over the next four years will continue to lose 10% of its value. That hurts!

Money Myths
"Your House is your Biggest Asset."
- Again, assets put money in your wallet every month in contrast to liabilities which take money out of your wallet every month. When buying a home for yourself to live in, and not as an investment with the purpose of getting a return on your money, your home by definition is a liability. Banks will tell you otherwise, but that's because they're loaning you a ton of money that you will be obligated to pay back in addition to all the interest that mounts up on top of it! Banks are making money from you, remember that.

"You should Always Buy a Car Brand New and Not Used."
- Simply not True. Although it's nice to buy a brand-new car, paying full price on something that loses value as soon as you drive it off the lot and continues to lose more value every time you drive it isn't the best idea. Buying used, reliable cars usually is a

much better option. Now and days, you can go to a dealership and buy a good, pre-certified, high quality, used car at a big discount when compared to buying a new car.

"It's Important to Keep up with the Trends."
- It really is not important to keep up with the trends. You don't need the new iPhone every time a new version is announced, you don't need a pair of overpriced Yeezy's to try and be the cool kid at school, and you don't need a huge Louis Vuitton purse to impress your friends. In fact, this is how a lot of very rich athletes and entertainers end up broke and in bankruptcy. They buy more expensive cars, more expensive homes, take more expensive vacations, and before they know it, they've maxed out their credit cards and have no money left in their bank account to pay any of it back.

Self-Reflection
1. Look at what your parents, your friends' parents, and adults around the neighborhood own. What items of their ownership can be

categorized as assets, and what items of their ownership can be categorized as liabilities?

2. What is something you have recently purchased and shortly after realized you really didn't need it? How did it feel at the time of purchase vs when you realized you shouldn't have bought it?

3. Next time you are at the point of purchase, how can you implement the asset vs liability mentality to help you determine whether to make the purchase or not?

CHOOSING PROFITS OVER WAGES

"WE'RE GROOMED FROM A VERY YOUNG AGE TO BECOME GOOD EMPLOYEES RATHER THAN BECOME GOOD INVESTORS AND ENTREPRENEURS."

As we've mentioned before, the school system is failing students each and every year by not adjusting the curriculum to reflect real world, practical problems. This has a carryover effect on a lot of other issues, including the topic of choosing profits or choosing wages. What does this mean? Most of us are taught to go to school, get good grades, so we can get into a good college, so at the end of everything we can land a good job. And by getting a good job what they really mean is to be paid a good, healthy salary so you can afford to have a good lifestyle. In other words, we're being groomed from a very young age to become good employees rather than become good investors and entrepreneurs. And unfortunately, being an employee does have its share of drawbacks.

What they don't tell you is that by getting a job and being an employee, you'll be earning a wage, which is typically taxed at the highest rate so even if you are earning a nice healthy salary your actual take home pay will be significantly less than what you earn. Not to mention that you'll have to answer to a boss, which you may or may not get along with, may have to drive in traffic for hours at a time to get to work, work with other staff members who may or may not make your job more stressful, and you'll have to deal with aspects of the job that you may not be too fond of like answering phone calls from difficult clients or having to constantly adhere to multiple deadlines. Let's be honest, at the end of the day you may not even like your job! You'll find yourself like millions of Americans across the country working a job that you hate simply because you have to pay your bills. Focusing your attention on earning profits over earning wages can save you from this life of complete misery.

Definitions & Examples
Wage: money that is paid or received for work or services, as by the hour, day, or week.

Example 1.

      Bob just finished up his senior year and is graduating from Arizona State University with a Bachelor of Arts degree in Communications. He logs on to Indeed and takes a look at the entry level jobs being offered and are available for him to apply to. He submits his resume to a call center, gets an interview, and lands the job. Bob is super excited, he'll be working 8am to 5pm Monday through Friday, will earn $17 per hour, will receive full health benefits after a 3-month probationary period, and will be eligible for a 3% yearly raise based on his performance.

      He does, however, realize his new job is nearly 35 miles away from where he currently lives, which with traffic, will take him over an hour and a half to get to the office and an hour and a half to get back home. Bob doesn't want the stress of having to drive in traffic every day, so he begins to look for an apartment to move closer to his new job. In doing so, he quickly becomes aware how expensive it really is to live independently. He does some math to figure out how much money he's actually making at his new job and how much he can actually afford for rent and still be able to pay for other bills.

$17 (dollars per hour) x 8 (hours per day) = $136 (dollars per day)

Bob is making $136 dollars per day.

$136 (dollars per day) x 5 (five days a week) = $680 (dollars per week)

Bob is making $680 per week.

$680 (dollars per week) x 2 (two weeks) = $1,360 (dollars bi-weekly)

Bob is making $1,360 dollars every two weeks.

$1,360 (dollars every two weeks) x 2 (per month) = $2,720 (dollars per month)

Bob is making $2,720 dollars per month.

$2,720 (dollars per month) x 12 (months per year) = $32,640 (dollars per year)

Bob is making $32,640 dollars per year, and this is before paying taxes and deductions which happen automatically when being paid by an employer. And that yearly 3% raise he was excited about:

$17 (dollars per hour) x .03 (percent yearly raise) = $0.51 (cents per year)

Turns out if he works really hard this year, he'll be able to earn a whopping $17.51 per hour next year. Not really significant at all. With having to pay for rent, making student loan payments, car payments, paying for car insurance, food, groceries, gas, going out with friends, going out with his girlfriend, taking family vacations, buying new clothes for work and for casual wear, and paying his cell phone bill he simply won't be able to pay for all these things at his current salary. And he can't ask for a raise yet because he just started his new job. Even if he did ask, getting a raise is up to senior management at the company and is not something that is under his control. Frustration and worry begin to set in for poor Bob.

Profits: can be returns, proceeds, or revenue generated.
Example 2.

Bob, in the example above, decides to figure out a way to make some extra income (develop a side hustle) rather than sit at home in sheer frustration. For much of his young life, he was a phenomenal soccer player and believes he has a lot of skill specific knowledge he can offer to young kids in the community. He creates a flyer offering soccer training services for kids ages 5 to 13 at $25 per hour, makes a hundred copies, and posts them up near three middle schools and two public parks. Within days, his phone starts ringing. Parents call in to inquire about his services and availability. Bob begins to schedule training sessions on both Saturday and Sunday mornings, and within weeks he has 5 clients, training each client once per week.

5 (total clients) x $25 (dollars per hour) = $125 (dollars per weekend)

Bob is now generating $125 dollars profit per weekend.

$125 (dollars per weekend) x 4 (weekends per month) = $500 per month (dollars per month)

Bob is making $500 dollars profit per month.

$500 (dollars per month) x 12 (months per year) = $6,000 (dollars per year)

And Bob will be making an extra $6,000 profit per year, which can be more if he takes on more clients as time progresses.

Bob absolutely loves being a soccer trainer and working with kids, gets to decide how much he wants to charge in terms of hourly rate, is his own boss and doesn't have to answer to anyone or ask permission to take time off, and the money he makes is all cash which means no taxes or deductions. It's awesome!

In both examples we can see the simple distinctions between earning profits and earning wages. When it comes to earning a wage, you don't get to decide how much money you make, you usually have a boss to answer to, and are forced to pay the government first in the form of taxes before you get paid. When it comes to earning profits you are usually your own boss, set your own rate, aren't capped to how much money you can make (the money you can make is theoretically unlimited), and depending on whether or not you decide to set up and operate as a legal business in your city and state you either won't pay taxes at all or pay taxes at the end of the year.

To apply it to Bob's example, he's making $500 per month and doesn't intend to take on many more clients and doesn't see the benefit of setting up a formal business, so he won't have to pay any taxes. However, if he at some point decides to take on more clients, offer training camps and other services that will earn him a lot more money, he may decide to start an actual company. In doing so, his business expenses may increase (buying equipment), but by becoming a business owner he'll be eligible for a lot of tax benefits and deductions that regular employees don't have access to. Furthermore, Bob will be able to take the profits being generated from his business to buy other assets that will generate him even more income.

Money Myths
"Just get a job, it's safer and more secure."
- This might have been true decades ago, but relatively speaking is no longer is true. Years ago, people were able to work a job for forty years, retire comfortably with a 401k, and have enough money to last them throughout retirement. Now and days this is not the case. The truth is that life in America has become extremely expensive, and by being an employee you're not really in control of your own future. And although we might feel that our job is secure, the fact of the matter is that your employer can fire and replace you with another employee in a matter of weeks.

"Starting a business is risky and costs a lot of money."
- Starting a business or a side hustle can be risky and cost a lot of money, but it doesn't have to. As we showed you in Bob's example, Bob didn't spend any money to start his side hustle. All he did was print flyers and post them around the neighborhood. It took more Guts than it required money to start his side hustle. And this is true for most small businesses. In general people are afraid to fail and use money and a barrage of other excuses as to why they can't start the business or side hustle they've always wanted to start. But if you can swallow your pride, realize you have nothing to lose and everything to gain, your earning potential can be unlimited.

Self-Reflection

1. When asked what you wanted to be when you grew up, what was your answer? Has that changed at all through the years? Why did you choose that profession?

2. Do some research. What are some pros and cons of forming a legal business? How many

different ways would you be able to structure a business?

3. Some side hustles and businesses aren't profitable. Why do you think some aren't profitable? What would be someone's goal for running a business or side hustle that isn't profitable?

THE MEANING OF BEING RICH vs WEALTHY

"MANY OF US GROW UP IDOLIZING PROFESSIONAL ATHLETES, FAMOUS CELEBRITIES, MOVIE ACTORS AND ACTRESSES, AND MUSIC ARTISTS BECAUSE OF THEIR FAME BUT EVEN MORE SO BECAUSE OF THEIR FORTUNE."

As kids, most of us grow up watching and idolizing professional athletes, famous celebrities, movie actors and actresses, music artists, and an array of other individuals who become popular by being covered by the media. Part of what we idolize about them is their fame, but usually the part we most admire about these individuals is the huge fortune they have amassed. We imagine what it's like to live in the life of one of these famous individuals, having seemingly a never-ending supply of money, carrying around stacks of cash, having huge resort like pools in our backyard, having multiple fast and fancy cars parked in the driveway of our mansion, wearing the latest trendy attire, and being covered in expensive diamonds and jewelry. And it's perfectly normal, as humans (especially as kids) we tend to think about and desire the things we don't possess. Moreover, because these famous individuals make life seem so amazing, we become incredibly curious and to a certain point envious of not being able to be in the same position those individuals are in.

But as we become young adults, should we still be financially idolizing these famous individuals? Are these individuals whom we admire considered to be rich? Or are they considered to be wealthy? Is there even a difference between the two? If there are differences between being rich and being wealthy, what are those differences? Should we aim to be rich? Or should we aim to be wealthy? When we're young we really don't put much thought into it, and usually use the terms rich and wealthy interchangeably. Understandably so, as both rich and wealthy refer to individuals who have a lot of money. But for purposes of clarity there are definitely some key distinctions between the two that you should be aware of. We'll get into some of those differences in our next section and present some examples that will help clear up any confusion relating to these two terms.

Definition & Examples

Rich: someone who is rich has a lot of money, has a high income, and usually lives a lavish and materialistic lifestyle, for example having huge mansions and exotic cars.

Example 1.

Jane and her husband Thomas are both architects and make an average yearly salary of about $90,000 dollars per year. That's a combined $180,000 dollars per year combined, not too shabby. Despite their high income, saving money is challenging for the two. They have two kids both attending private school, Jane drives a new Mercedes Benz while Thomas drives a new BMW, they bought a beautiful home in the heart of Silicon Valley California, and take at least two vacations per year, staying at only the best hotels of course. Their expenses are so high that on a yearly basis they are only able to save a combined $10,000 dollars per year.

Jane also plays the Lotto at least twice a month with hopes to win big one day. Much to her surprise that one day actually does arrive. She sees the winning numbers on her computer screen, double checks her ticket, and realizes she has just won 2.5 million dollars! She and her husband Thomas are both ecstatic and decide together to take the lump sum of money. They calculate that after taxes they will have an estimated $1.8 million dollars in cash to spend as they please. It's more money than they've ever imagined having, are now rich, and it's awesome!

After receiving the money, they sell their house and move into a bigger, more expensive home worth 1.4 million dollars, however they don't buy it outright with cash and instead only put 10% down payment ($140,000 dollars). They also decide they both need newer cars, a range rover and a Tesla, a combined purchase of about $190,000 dollars but again they opt to finance instead of paying all cash. They also go on a shopping spree buying new clothes and shoes for themselves and their kids, Jane upgrades her wedding ring, Thomas buys season tickets to watch the Golden State Warriors, and they plan on taking a two-month vacation to Europe during the summer when the kids are on summer break. Their new life is amazing and both Jane and Thomas feel blessed to be alive.

Wealthy: someone who is wealthy owns assets that pay for their lifestyle, has the ability to pass on their wealth to future generations, and has the knowledge to create and multiply money.

Example 2.

Phil and Monique have been married for over twenty years and have worked at the same jobs for approximately the same amount of time. Phil works as a Mechanical Engineer taking home around $80,000 dollars per year, while Monique works at a health clinic as a Licensed Vocational Nurse (LVN) and has an average salary of $50,000 dollars per year. With both incomes combined, both Phil and Monique take home approximately $130,000 dollars each year, enough for a decently nice lifestyle. Phil and Monique, however, are very conscious of their spending and have made the decision to live way below their means. They work in downtown Orlando Florida but live in a modest home in the suburbs thirty minutes away, commute to work together in the same car (Honda Civic) they've had for years, opted to send their kids to public schools instead of private schools, and take two vacations per year but shop for bargain prices online.

Both Monique and Phil are able to save about $40,000 a year of their earned income, which is great. But through the years they've also developed side streams of income, invested in the stock market, and invested in real estate which has allowed them to build a steady flow of passive and portfolio income. Phil has published multiple books on Amazon which earns him nearly $1,200 dollars in royalties every month, and Monique has created an online course teaching young individuals the ins and outs of being an LVN which nets her nearly $800 dollars a month. Both of their small businesses are completely automated. In terms of real estate, they've been able to acquire one new investment property every three years, which at this point is now equal to seven properties total. Each property is cashflow positive of about $450 dollars per month:

$450 (cashflow per month) x 7 (total properties) = $3,150 (total cashflow per month)

In total they are able to bring in $3,150 dollars a month in rental income. When it comes to the stock market, both Phil and Monique have continuously invested in companies they are familiar with whether their price in stock was going up or down. Wal-Mart, Coca Cola, AT&T, and Johnson and Johnson, are all companies they have acquired stock in. They have however never sold any of their stock despite huge amounts of appreciation, and instead focus on holding long term and re-investing the dividends their stocks pay. In total dividends both Phil and Monique generate approximately $2,200 a month, which is amazing.

They're in such a good place financially that they plan on retiring from their jobs in three years once their primary residence is paid off. Phil will be 48 years old, and Monique will be 46, both will be retiring almost twenty years early! And better yet, they will be completely self-reliant and have no need for social security or government assistance. Furthermore, their kids will be living away from home in college, tuition being paid for by passive and portfolio income, and Phil and Monique plan on traveling around the world for months which is something they've always wanted to do.

Considering our first example, our lotto winners Jane and Thomas, how long do you believe the 2.5 million dollars will actually last them? With their spending habits we can infer that it won't be very long at all. They are considered what is to be rich, and if you were to judge a book by its cover you may believe they had a never-ending supply of money, but that just simply isn't the case. Although they were handed millions of dollars, at the end of the day it is a finite amount of money that will run out relatively quickly if they don't take control of their expenses. This is what happens to many professional athletes, actors, and entertainers whom we idolize growing up. They make millions and millions of dollars each and every year, but also spend millions and millions of dollars each and every year. Saving and investing money for the future doesn't ever cross their mind. And guess what happens when those large sums of money they were making slowly start to deteriorate? Their high consumption lifestyle all comes crashing down as well. They can no longer afford to live in their huge mansions, drive their top-of-the-line vehicles, take extravagant vacations, and lose their expensive diamonds and jewelry. Without sugar coating it, they go broke!

If the 2.5-million-dollar lotto winnings had instead been given to a couple like Phil and Monique how do you believe that money would've been used? If we had to guess the lotto winnings would probably go straight into their savings and investments. Why, Phil and Monique understand that it's not about looking or being rich, it's more about accumulating long term wealth that will allow them to detach themselves from the daily grind (which we'll talk more about in a later section). Having the ability to control money rather than letting money control them is often what separates the rich with high expenses from the wealthy who live below their means. People's money problems don't go away by being given large sums of money. In fact, it may actually make their money problems worse. You see, individuals with large amounts of debt and lots of unnecessary expenses don't need millions of dollars, they need financial education. Without financial education any amount of money they are given will quickly evaporate due to their spending habits and lack of skills when it comes to keeping and multiplying money. As we've mentioned before, what's the benefit of making a lot of money if we aren't able to keep it?

Money Myths
"Winning the Lotto is my best chance of getting rich and having a lot of money."
- If your plan to make a lot of money includes winning the lotto, you're going to be immensely disappointed. Your chances of winning the jackpot are estimated to be approximately 1 in 14,000,000 (fourteen million), which is extremely low to say the least. Your best chance of making a lot of money is through entrepreneurship, becoming a business owner, and making sound investments. Relying on complete luck, which is what the lottery is, to make money will get you nowhere.

"I can't wait twenty or thirty years to be rich, I need to get rich now."
- Building wealth takes time, there's no way around it unless you inherit a ton of money from a relative. Even then, someone who inherits a large sum of money may blow right through it as we've already talked about. The truth is that in order to make a lot of

money and learn how to keep that money first must start with having the correct mindset. This mindset is developed over time usually by making mistakes, reading, research, due diligence, and self-education. It's great to have motivation, but it's equally important to be patient and maintain the vision of your long-term goal even through obstacles and roadblocks.

Self-Reflection

1. Do some research on a few famous individuals whom you idolize. Are they investing their money? If so, what are they investing in? How will they continue to have an income even after retirement?

2. Make a list of three individuals who were once rich and have now gone bankrupt. What took place that led to their bankruptcy?

3. How will you avoid making the same mistakes rich individuals have made that has led to them being broke?

OPPORTUNITY DURING RECESSION

"ONE OF THE MOST FAMOUS QUOTES MADE BY ARGUABLY THE GREATEST INVESTOR OF ALL TIME, WARREN BUFFET… "BE FEARFUL WHEN OTHERS ARE GREEDY, AND GREEDY WHEN OTHERS ARE FEARFUL."

Recession can be a blessing in disguise in terms of making money and long-term wealth accumulation. Yes, you read that right. It may seem counterintuitive because whenever we hear about recession from family, friends, and the media we're usually hearing the words "disaster, financial hardship, people losing homes, people losing their jobs, foreclosure, and filing for bankruptcy." But again, part of becoming a successful entrepreneur and investor involves thinking differently than most of the general population. This ties in perfectly with one of the most famous quotes made by arguably the greatest investor of all time, Warren Buffet… "Be Fearful when others are Greedy, and Greedy when others are Fearful."

It's important to constantly be looking at situations from the other side of the coin. Where most see problems you must see solutions, where most see a lack of resources you must see an abundance of resources, and where most see a lack of opportunities you must see a never-ending supply of opportunities. When individuals prepare for a recession, as we all should be doing by educating ourselves, an incredible number of opportunities present themselves to make money and become wealthy. These opportunities are available to everyone, but only those who have trained and prepared themselves to see and take advantage of these opportunities will be able to capitalize.

Definitions & Examples

Recession: when the overall economy significantly declines for an extended period of time (at least six months). In short, unemployment rates rise, wages decrease, the stock market crashes, real estate prices drop dramatically, and consumer spending also significantly decreases.

Example 1.

Jason is 25 years old and has been living with his parents rent free in order to save money. He decided not to attend college and has been working two jobs ever since he graduated high school. To date, he's been able to save ten thousand dollars per year since he was eighteen years old.

$10,000 (per year) x 7 (years) = $70,000 (in total savings)

He's saved a total of seventy thousand dollars. He's also been keeping up with economic data and feels that in general both the stock market and real estate market are overpriced/overbought, and the amount of debt is reaching alarmingly high levels across the country. He doesn't believe this can go on for too much longer and thinks there's a correction in the market coming soon.

Jason was right, two and a half years later recession hits, to most without warning. People can't afford to pay back their debt, consumer spending slows dramatically, people begin losing their jobs as employers begin to lay people off, home prices dip, and the stock market begins to crash. Panic is in the air as most people have overleveraged debt and have failed to save money in case of an emergency like this.

Jason on the other hand, now has a total of ninety-five thousand dollars he's saved up. One of his jobs cut his hours back by a few, but this doesn't significantly affect his income. In fact, he isn't scared and isn't in panic mode at all. The very opposite in fact, he's enticed by the incredibly low home and stock prices. Homes that were once worth four and five hundred thousand dollars are now being sold and foreclosed for half the price, and companies that were trading in the stock market at incredibly high prices are now listed at a fraction of the price.

Jason knows the correction will bottom out at some point, and the economy will again rise and expand to new highs (because history shows us that it ALWAYS does).

He makes his move and buys thirty thousand dollars-worth of stocks but only in companies he knows have a solid balance sheet and will continue to grow. Apple, Google, Facebook, Verizon, Amazon, Exxon Mobil, and more are companies he adds to his portfolio, again at a very low price in comparison to when the market was overbought. He also goes online and does some research on the local real estate market. Homes in the city where he lives that were once selling for 340, 350, and 360 thousand dollars just a year ago are now listed for sale at 180, 190, and 200 hundred thousand dollars. He gives himself the green light, as again he knows the real estate market will eventually bounce back and acquires a two bedroom 2 bath home for $180,000 dollars (putting twenty percent down). He plans on living in the home for a few years, possibly renting the extra room to a friend, and slowly working on renovations so he can sell or rent at a higher price point when the market rises again.

For people who lack financial education, Jason might seem as if he's losing his marbles. Afterall, who in their right mind would be buying and acquiring assets when those asset prices are crashing to record setting lows? Which at face value makes sense, but this is not how financially savvy individuals think. In Jason's example he had saved up for 9-10 years and had a little over $90,000 dollars at his disposal. He invested wisely, and because he did so, he just about guarantees his income and net worth to increase exponentially as the market recovers. Now, can you imagine how much money high net worth, savvy investors who have one million, five million, or ten million dollars at their disposal can make during times of recession? A ton! And this is one of the very reasons why "the rich get richer, and the poor get poorer."

It's simply a matter of switching your mindset and seeing the world from a different perspective. Again, going back to the wise words from the great Warren Buffet "Be fearful when others are greedy, and greedy when others are fearful." When everyone else is buying homes, buying stocks, and overleveraging debt to finance their purchases is when you should be cautious and hesitant to follow the crowd, in other words you should be doing the opposite. Although it may seem that you should be spending money because everyone else is spending money, that is simply not the case. We'll end this section with a simple comparison… When we walk into a shoe store or a clothing store and see "ON SALE" signs in front of items that we like, are we more enticed to buy? Well, the items are on sale so we should take advantage of the low prices, right? The same is the case during recessions and economic hard times. Homes and stocks literally go "ON SALE" but most people will opt not to buy.

Money Myths
"It's impossible to predict when the next recession will happen."
-It's extremely difficult to predict exactly when the next recession will be, especially because we usually don't know we're in a recession until we're actually in it. However, through financial education we can see a clearer picture as to when our economy is headed for trouble. By looking at and keeping up with key economic variables (unemployment, real estate, stock market, wages, interest rates, etc.), we can determine the overall health of the economy and at the very least have a sense of the direction we're headed in.

"Recessions are extremely rare and therefore I shouldn't worry about them happening."
-Our last recession (at the time of writing) was back in 2008 when the real estate bubble burst, and the recession before that took place way back in 2001. So, for most of you, you've only been exposed to two declines in the market, though you were likely very

young and didn't realize what was actually happening. The fact of the matter is that recessions are a normal part of our economy and a normal part of our business cycles and will happen again repeatedly throughout your adult life. Because of this, you should prepare yourself as best as possible to survive these financial hard times.

Self-Reflection

1. Considering the current state of our economy, when do you predict the next recession to be? How will you prepare?

2. What opportunities will arise when the next recession takes place? How will you take advantage of the opportunities that may arise?

Phase Four: Financial Freedom & Abundance

Individuals in the phase of financial freedom and abundance:

☐ Are no longer part of the Rat Race and have the option to retire when they want.

☐ Are generating enough income to pay for their lifestyle, unexpected expenses, and extravagant luxuries.

☐ Are able to continuously donate and contribute financially to provide resources and opportunities for others.

☐ Have accrued generational wealth.

CREATING MULTIPLE STREAMS OF INCOME

"BY LEVERAGING THESE DEVICES AND THE ACCESSIBILITY OF THE ONLINE WORLD, YOU CAN VERY EASILY LEARN TO MAKE MONEY FROM THE COMFORT OF YOUR OWN HOME."

If you were to go up to ten people randomly at the supermarket, in and around your neighborhood, or at the mall and asked them.... "How can I make more money?" You're pretty much guaranteed to get one of two answers:

1. Get another job that pays you more money.
    Or
2. Get a part-time job, either working nights or on the weekends, on top of your full-time job. In other words, have two jobs.

And this isn't necessarily wrong advice, those two options will without a doubt allow you to make more money, but it highlights the issue of how people are absolutely clueless about all the other possible opportunities that are seemingly at our fingertips when it comes to building additional income streams. Getting a higher paying job or getting two jobs for that matter are NOT the only ways you can increase your income. There are literally hundreds, maybe thousands, of other ways to make money, and with technology evolving and adapting every day the possibilities only continue to expand.

We're living in a time where you have access to an unlimited amount of information via your cell phone, iPads, tablets, and laptop computers. By leveraging these devices and the accessibility of the online world, you can very easily learn to make money from the comfort of your own home. You can build your own online store, you can sell items on platforms such as Esty and Amazon, you can learn to buy and trade stock and stock options through a brokerage, you can make money off of advertisements on platforms such as YouTube and Instagram, you can become an online marketer and offer services for new companies, and the list of possibilities can go on and on. Let's explore further what types of income streams are available for you to take advantage of.

Definitions & Examples

Earned Income: the income or compensation you receive from a job, usually in the form of wages, salary, or tips.

Example 1.

The majority of Americans work Monday through Friday (five days a week) for eight hours a day, which equals forty total hours per week. In return for the hours we work, we receive a paycheck every two weeks (some of us are paid hourly and some of us are paid salary). In other words, we're trading our time for money.

Portfolio Income: income or payment you receive coming from investments such as capital gains, interest, royalties, and dividends.

Example 2.

If you were to buy 100 shares of Verizon (at the time of writing 1 share of Verizon stock is roughly $57) you would be paid dividends once a quarter (every three months). In Verizon's case, they pay their shareholders dividends on February 1st, May 1st, August 1st, and November 1st every year. Buying 100 shares would cost you $5,700:

100 (total shares bought) x $57 (stock price) = $5,700 total investment.

The current dividend yield is roughly 4.2% per year, meaning every year you would earn $239.4 (in dividend payments alone).

$5,700 (total investment) x 0.042 (dividend yield per year) = $239.4 (dividend payments per year)

If we wanted to find out how much we would make in dividends every quarter, we would simply divide by 4 (4 quarters in a year).

$239.4 (dividend payments per year) / 4 (four quarters per year) = $59.85 (dividend payments per quarter)

You would be paid $59.85 per quarter (every three months) simply for holding the stock! Again, we are not taking into consideration that the stock price will likely appreciate over time and that a company like Verizon tends to increase their dividend yield every year.

Passive Income: income you receive from rental property, or a business arrangement in which you are not actively involved in.

Example 3.

 If you were to purchase an investment property where your total monthly payment including mortgage, insurance, property taxes (etc.) came out to a total of $1,200 per month, and you turned around and rented the property to someone else for $1,450 per month, that would mean you'd have an extra $250 per month in your wallet (each and every month). $1,450 (monthly payment for the renter) – $1,200 (your total monthly payment) = $250 (your profit every month)

 This $250 profit is considered passive income as you're not actively involved in the business (not trading your time for money). Furthermore, rental rates tend to increase every year, which would allow you to increase your earnings each and every year.

 This idea of being able to make money without having to go to work sounds almost foreign. Most of us are taught by our teachers and our parents, which are authority figures we tend to take life and career advice from, to go to school in order to get a good desk job and sit in a nice office. But in doing so most of us miss the powerful opportunity to have multiple streams of income in the form of passive and portfolio compensation. It's accessible to all of us and is something we can and should take advantage of. Let's consider the following statistics:

According to a study by Gallup in 2017, it's estimated that over 75% percent of Americans hate their jobs and something like 90% percent of workers worldwide find their jobs to be a source of stress and frustration rather than enjoyment and fulfillment. Those numbers are staggering, but not surprising. If we really sit down and think about it, how many times have we heard our parents, friend's parents, and adults around us complain day in and day out about how they hate their boss, about how they hate to drive in traffic each and every day, about how underpaid they are, about how they hate dealing with customers, about not having enough vacation time, and about being fed up with having to deal with the daily grind? This very conversation happens all too often and is unfortunate to say the least. But this doesn't have to be your reality.

Like we've mentioned before, there's nothing wrong with having a job.... but along with having a job and using the income from your job you should put in the extra work to build additional streams of income.

What do you have to lose? A few hours of sleep a week? Would you really be up for working a job for forty years, deal with all the hardships mentioned in the previous paragraph, and hope and pray you have enough to retire when you're sixty-five years old? It's time to take control of your own life and your own finances. You are literally living in the best time in human history when it comes to building wealth. Utilize your time efficiently, take advantage of the information you have at your fingertips, develop your skills as an investor and an entrepreneur, and watch your income skyrocket!

One final thought, the average millionaire has a total of 7 streams of income. Millionaires and other high net worth individuals don't depend on their job to get them what they want in life. They invest in stocks, they purchase real estate properties, they sell their ideas through patents, they earn royalties from products, and they build businesses to help them not only reach but surpass their financial goals.

Money Myths
"Don't plan on becoming rich by building a business. Most businesses fail."

- Although it's true that most businesses fail within the first three years, by no means does that mean you should give up. When it comes to building a business and additional streams of income, you will likely encounter difficulties and experience some form of failure. Failure is actually a normal part of success. Despite this, however, a lot of people will give up at the first sight of failure, which causes them to sell themselves short of a possible breakthrough and success. If instead you keep at it, with each mistake and failure will come a lesson that will pay you dividends in the future.

"Never work for Free! Always make sure you're compensated with money when you work."
- There may be some confusion here, but this is false. When you are young you should set priority to learning high income skills, not necessarily to earning a paycheck. If you come across an individual who owns multiple businesses and has made successful investments, instead of asking that person to teach you his/her secrets, ask that person if you can work for them for free. Why would that person share their hard-earned lessons with you? What incentive does

he or she have to give you free information that they likely worked very hard to attain? None. But who wouldn't want to have someone work for free for them? By working for free it's a win for them and it's a win for you because you'll have the opportunity to build a good relationship and learn from someone who has attained something that you want.

Self-Reflection

1. What are you passionate about? In what ways do you believe you can monetize your passion?

2. How do you plan on using your earned income to funnel money and grow your portfolio and passive income streams?

3. What platforms do you use on a regular basis (Facebook, Instagram, YouTube, etc.)? Can you see the opportunities in building an income stream through those platforms? If yes, in what ways?

INVESTING IN THE STOCK MARKET

"GENERAL RULE OF THUMB YOU SHOULD ALWAYS REMEMBER…IF IT SOUNDS TOO GOOD TO BE TRUE, IT PROBABLY IS."

Most of you have heard about the stock market at some point or another. Whether it's from an online article explaining how one person got rich off of investing in certain stocks, whether it's from social media reading a post about Warren Buffet (one of the greatest investors of all time) and one of his famous quotes about investing, or by simply turning on the television and hearing a financial reporter say, "the Dow Jones is down 300 points since Monday of last week." There tends to be a lot of noise surrounding the stock market as it is often used as an indicator of how healthy our economy is at a given time. And if you've never heard of stocks and the stock market before, then welcome to one of the most important investing vehicles you will ever come across in your lifetime.

Lots of money and wealth can be generated from stocks and the stock market. However, in order to be profitable and generate wealth in the stock market you must have the right knowledge and a good strategy in place to have the best chance of winning and being profitable. And frankly, coming across good investing advice is hard to come by. In reality, there is a ton of information online about how to invest in stocks and what stocks in particular you should buy, but you must be aware that not all information is good information. In fact, there is an unbelievable amount of bad and flat-out wrong information out there being provided to young and inexperienced investors. Tips including how to get rich quick, tips on what high risk penny stocks you should invest in that are sure to blow up, and tips on how to time and beat the overall market.

A general rule of thumb you should always remember…. "If it sounds too good to be true, it probably is." The fact of the matter is that it takes time for investments to appreciate in value, it's not typically something that can happen overnight. Before you begin investing in anything related to the stock market, you should absolutely do your due diligence and learn the language of the stock market. In the next section you'll be introduced to some of the most basic financial terms typically used when referencing stocks and the stock market, but by no means is it an exhaustive list of what you need to know before deciding to pick and buy stocks.

Definitions & Examples

Market Capitalization- the market value of a company represented in dollar amounts. This figure can be calculated by multiplying a company's outstanding shares by the current market price of one share.

Example 1.

      If the company Montview Inc was trading at $50 per share and had 1 billion outstanding shares, $50 x 1 Billion shares = $50 Billion in market capitalization.

Large Cap Stocks- a company with a market capitalization of more than 10 billion.

Example 2.

      At the time of writing, Apple has a market capitalization (is worth) of $909 Billion, making it a large cap stock.

Mid Cap Stocks- a company with a market capitalization between 2 billion and 10 billion.
Example 3.

    At the time of writing, United Rentals has a market capitalization (is worth) of $9.39 Billion, making it a mid-cap stock.

Small Cap Stocks- a company with a market capitalization of less than 2 billion.
Example 4.

    At the time of writing, KushCo Holdings has a market capitalization (is worth) $533 Million, making it a small cap stock.

Fundamental Analysis- this measures the intrinsic value of a stock. This takes into account a given company's earnings, expenses, assets, and liabilities (just to name a few).
Example 5.

    Miranda is looking to invest $2,000 into Verizon stock. She looks and studies Verizon's quarterly and yearly financials, including how much money is generated, how much is profit, how much they spend on supplies and expenses, how much debt the company has, and what the company is projecting to make the following quarter (just to name a few criteria). After analyzing Verizon's financials, Miranda feels that Verizon is headed in the right direction and is positioning itself to make more money and be a lot more profitable in the future, not to mention that they also pay a nice dividend every quarter. She decides to buy $2,000 worth of stock and hold it without selling for the next few years.

Technical Analysis- this takes into account the stock's price and volume. Investors using technical analysis use stock patterns and trends that suggest what a stock will do in the future.
Example 6.

Billy is looking to make a quick profit on Aurora Cannabis stock. He looks at Aurora's stock price chart and realizes that it's been on an upwards trajectory for the past few days and is on pace to hit $11 per share which will be the highest the stock price has ever been. He decides to buy 40 shares at $9.50 per share, which is a total investment of $380. He again, hopes to sell all 40 of his shares at $11 per share, which would net him a $60 dollar profit.

40 (shares) x 11 (expected stock price) = $440 (expected value)

$440 (expected value of holdings) - $380 (current value of holdings) = $60 (profit)

Again, the terms and examples provided to you in the previous section are ONLY an INTRODUCTION to the world of stocks and the stock market. It's not a comprehensive list of everything you should know before taking the leap of faith in buying and selling stocks. An important point you should also realize is that becoming a good stock market investor requires a series of skills that you without a doubt CAN learn. It's in actuality a lot like participating and becoming good at a given sport.

When we watch someone who is really good at basketball, really good at soccer, really good at volleyball, really good at softball or baseball, or whatever sport it may be, we see them in sheer amazement of how they're able to collectively use their skills and compete at a high level. However, for almost all of these really good athletes, it didn't start out that way. For the vast majority of these athletes, the first time they participated in their given sport they weren't very good at all. They knew every little about what it took to be a good player, they didn't have the skill set in place, they didn't have the right mindset, and they had no idea what it took to win. But through the years, they practiced, and practiced, and practiced, became students of their given sport, kept learning, kept being coachable, watched and learned from athletes that were better than them, and by not giving up eventually became good athletes themselves.

Becoming a successful and profitable investor is something that you can totally learn and is possible for you, not something that people are born with. Yes some people may have a higher Intelligence Quotient (I.Q.), may come from rich families, may be better at math, and may have the networks in place that would make it easier for them to get better investment advice. But if you put in the work and persevere through your initial failures, you'll undoubtedly learn how to earn steady profits from the stock market.

Money Myths
"Investing in the Stock Market is Risky."
- Yes, there is always some level of risk when investing in the stock market. However, that risk can

be very minimal when compared to the potential upside if you really study hard and do your homework. We'll even take it a step further and say it's more risky to NOT invest in the stock market than it is TO invest in the stock market. How so? If people expect to work 40 years at a job that doesn't pay well in the first place, choose not to invest because it's too risky, and expect to have enough money to retire comfortably will sadly be in for a rude awakening. Investing allows for an additional stream of income that can evolve into massive amounts with time and patience.

"I can become very Rich very Fast by buying and selling stocks."
- Many individuals throughout history have made a ton of money by buying and selling stocks. However, an extremely small percentage of these individuals have been able to do it quickly. We hate to sound like a broken record, but it truly does take time and patience to make money in the stock market. Especially when first starting out, because just like anything else you'll need to learn from trial and error which means you'll likely lose money before you're able to make money.

"Only really smart people can make money in the Stock Market."

- There are a lot of intelligent and financially savvy individuals who make money in the stock market, this is true. Yet there are also many intelligent and financially savvy individuals who are NOT making any money in the stock market. Without a good strategy, without a good plan, without the correct knowledge to weed out good investments from bad investments, incredibly intelligent individuals can lose money in the stock market too. In fact, it happens every day. Truth be told it's not about how smart you are, it's more about putting in the work to become a good and financially sound investor. Making money through investing is a learnable skill, not a personality characteristic individuals are born with.

Self-Reflection

1. What investment advice have you received in the past in relation to stocks and the stock market? Did this advice come from a reliable source?

2. If you had $10,000 to invest in the stock market today, what stocks would you invest in? Why would you invest in these stocks in particular? Do any of your investment picks have commonalities between them?

3. How do you believe the stock market relates to the overall economy? How do adults generally react when the stock market is on an upward trajectory, and how do adults generally react when the stock market is on a downward trajectory? What emotions do you believe are involved when in a growing market versus in a down market?

INVESTING IN THE REAL ESTATE MARKET

"IT'S ESTIMATED THAT OVER THE COURSE OF THE LAST TWO HUNDRED YEARS, OVER 90% PERCENT OF THE WORLD'S MILLIONAIRES HAVE BEEN CREATED BY INVESTING IN REAL ESTATE."

It's estimated that over the course of the last two hundred years, over 90% percent of the world's millionaires have been created by investing in real estate. An incredible statistic that clearly highlights the power of using real estate to build and accumulate wealth and financial resources. Why is real estate so powerful you might be wondering? Well, if we view real estate from an entrepreneurial perspective, it becomes evident that real estate solves a very simple problem in the marketplace…the never-ending need for Housing. Everyone needs a place to live, and as the population continues to increase on a year-by-year basis, there will be an ever increasing need for housing which of course will continue to drive home and rent prices up. This will put an increasing amount of pressure on the development and construction of more homes and apartment buildings.

It should be noted however that there are several different ways to be involved and make money from real estate. Let's go over two of the more popular avenues that you've likely seen in articles, and television and consider a few different examples illustrating the benefits of each option.

Definition & Examples

Flipping: when an investor buys a property with the intention of re-selling it for a profit.

Example 1.

Malcolm is twenty years old and lives in the outskirts of New Orleans Louisiana. He's been working full time as a Life Insurance Agent for the past two years and has been saving as much money as he possibly can. He's been saving very aggressively to partner up with his Uncle Bryan who buys and flips homes for a living. His Uncle Bryan told him if he's able to save up at least $25,000 to invest he'd allow Malcolm to be part of his next real estate flip. He does caution Malcolm however and explains that flipping can get expensive very quickly.

Malcolm is up for the challenge, finally reaches twenty-five thousand dollars in savings, and teams up with his uncle. They go to the bank together, get approved for a $400,000 loan, search for a property in distress (needing repairs), and make an offer of $220,000 on a 4-bedroom 3 bath nearby home that was listed for sale for $280,000. His uncle Bryan negotiates and is able to buy the home for $240,000, which he believes to be a good deal. He estimates that they'll need to spend approximately $60,000 dollars on repairs (demolition, bathroom repairs, kitchen repairs, flooring, etc.), and if done right they would be able to sell the home for a grand total of $420,000 dollars. That's a profit of:

$240,000 (purchase price) + $60,000 (total repairs) = $300,000 (total investment)

$420,000 (ideal selling price) - $300,00 (total investment) = $120,000 (total profit)

If all goes well, they will profit one hundred and twenty thousand dollars in total! Split between the two that would be sixty thousand dollars for each. They do, however, need to get started on repairs and renovations right away because payments toward the mortgage begin immediately the following month, which will eat away at their profit the longer the repairs and renovations take to get done.

Landlord: the owner of a property who turns around and rents or leases that property to a business or an individual.

Example 2.

Julie has been earning a good salary for the past five years, making approximately $85,000 per year living near Phoenix Arizona. She's kept her expenses exceptionally low and has been able to save twenty thousand dollars per year for the past five years, meaning she's stacked up about one hundred thousand dollars total (which she's very excited about). She's interested in investing in real estate to earn some passive income as a landlord. She finds a real estate agent whom she trusts and finds a beautiful 3 bedroom 2 bath single family home listed at $250,000 dollars not too far from where she currently lives. Julie puts in a bid of $225,000 which luckily gets accepted by the seller. Julie puts down twenty percent:

$225,000 (purchase price) x 0.2 (twenty percent down) = $45,000 (total down payment)

Her total down payment is forty-five thousand dollars, and she'll finance the remaining $180,000 dollars through a bank loan. According to her bank her monthly payment including principle, interest, taxes, and insurance will be $1,100 dollars. This is great because Julie believes she can lease the home to a family for $1,500 per month.

$1,500 (rental rate) - $1,100 (monthly payment) = $400 (monthly profit)

Julie will be making a monthly profit of four hundred dollars per month, or:

$400 (monthly profit) x 12 (months per year) = $4,800 (profit per year)

$4,800 dollars in passive income per year. This is wonderful! If all goes well Julie plans on purchasing a new investment property and repeating this same process every two to three years.

Both Malcolm and Julie are well on their way to becoming successful real estate investors and entrepreneurs. Malcolm is looking forward to a nice hefty profit from a home flip, while Julie is looking forward to recurring deposits of income to her bank account at the end of every month. Although both flipping and being a landlord are great options for getting involved in real estate, which of the two is the better option? That honestly depends on who you ask. Successful flippers can generate massive profits every year, but also must put in a ton of hard work and heavy manual labor to repair these distressed properties in order to have potential buyers pay top dollar. Also, if they were to stop flipping homes their stream of income also stops, since their income is dependent on them actually having to work. Being a landlord on the other hand allows for more freedom. Tenants pay the mortgage and a little extra so the landlord can make a nice profit every month. It's a form of passive income and does not require the landlord to show up for work or do any manual labor. Landlords can literally be on vacation for months on end and still earn profits.

Furthermore, the risks when it comes to flipping and leasing are very different. When flipping a property, you may run into foundational issues that may cost much more than you anticipated and take longer to repair. If these repairs take long enough, you can quickly run out of money and risk having to ask for more money from the bank, friends, or relatives, putting yourself in even more debt. When being a landlord, in order to make a profit you must be able to get tenants to sign your lease and occupy the home. If the home itself isn't up to date, isn't in a desirable location, or isn't visually appealing, you run the risk of not being able to lease it for the amount you were aiming for or not being able to lease the property out at all for months on end. This of course will have a negative effect on your bottom dollar.

To conclude, both flipping and being a landlord are excellent ways of investing in real estate and generating income, but as with most forms of investing both come with their own share of risks. It's important to be educated and do your share of due diligence to minimize those risks, understand the tax benefits and liability, and maximize profits for the long term.

Money Myths
"Flipping distressed properties is too much work and requires too much money."
-Being able to flip properties that require repairs and renovations does require a lot of hard work and money, but with the right knowledge you can leverage using other people's money to pay for those

renovations and repairs. By teaming up with a mentor, working with an experienced house flipper, and/or having connections with investors can give you access to large sums of money. You can then turn around and use this money to flip homes, and once you're able to sell those renovated properties you can pay off the people that helped you, with prearranged payment rates, and still keep a healthy profit for yourself. You'll just need to make sure the numbers work for you so you can end up with a profit rather than end up with a financial loss.

"Being a landlord sucks. You have to deal with crazy phone calls from tenants every time there's an issue with the property."
-Being a landlord can suck, but it doesn't always. There are a few ways you can avoid phone calls from complaining tenants at unpredictable hours of the night. One, you can make sure your property is up to date with repairs, and everything is functioning as it should before you list it for rent. Two, you can hire a property manager to deal with all issues related to the property. This option may take a bite out of your profits, but if you're adamant about not dealing with

tenants this might be your best option. It may also be your best option once you own several properties (so you don't have to manage them all). Three, you can be very selective as to who you allow to lease your property. Conducting thorough interviews, calling references, setting strict qualifying income requirements, and not allowing pets are all examples of how you can be selective as to who you allow to lease your property.

Self-Reflection

1. How do you plan on getting started in real estate? Would you look to form a partnership with someone? Why or why not?

2. Presently, in what areas would you invest in? Why would you invest in these areas?

3. In the future, what areas do you see having the most upside for investing? Why do you see these areas as having the most upside?

THE POWER OF COMPOUND INTEREST

"THE CONCEPT OF COMPOUNDING IS OFTEN COMPARED TO WHAT'S KNOWN AS THE SNOWBALL EFFECT."

We've discussed interest and how paying interest can negatively impact your financial picture, but now let's talk about how you can get on the other side of the coin and earn interest, particularly compound interest. Earning interest on your money is awesome but allowing that money you earn in interest to compound over time is incredibly powerful. The concept of compounding is often compared to what many of us know to be "The Snowball Effect." For those of you that aren't familiar with the concept of the snowball effect, imagine rolling up a snowball in your hands, going to the top of a mountain, and releasing that snowball allowing it to roll down all the way to the bottom.

In theory, the snowball would be relatively small in size when you first throw it because it's something you made in your hands. But as it continues to roll down the mountain top it continues to gain speed, traction, and momentum while at the same time increase in size as it builds up with more and more snow. Before you know it the small snowball you rolled down the mountain top becomes a huge ball of snow with the potential to start an avalanche. Now, imagine the same concept but instead of a snowball it's with money. A small and almost insignificant deposit you make into an account or investment that you allow to compound over time can become a very large sum of money. Let's take a look at the examples that follow and compare simple interest, which is what most you are familiar with, and compound interest, which is what investors use to accumulate massive wealth.

Definitions & Examples
Simple Interest: interest that is calculated based on the original contribution to a savings account or the principal portion of a loan. Simple interest does not compound over time.
Example 1.

Nicholas has a rich uncle who suddenly dies of a heart attack. In his uncle's will, Nicholas and his sister Becky are each to be gifted twenty-five thousand dollars to spend as they please. They both would rather save the money for a rainy day and opt not to spend it but instead put it into an account that earns interest over the years. That way they can earn money on their money. Smart idea! Becky chooses to put her money into an account that earns at a rate of 7% simple interest, and the following is what she can expect to earn back over the course of 25 years if she doesn't touch the money and leaves it in the account.

Interest rate: 7%	Simple interest
Initial deposit	$25,000
Year 1	$26,750
Year 5	$33,750
Year 10	$42,500
Year 15	$51,250
Year 20	$60,000
Year 25	$68,750

As you can see, Becky's account grows to sixty-eight thousand, seven hundred and fifty dollars over the course of twenty-five years! That's great, she more than doubles her money without having to do any work.

Compound Interest: interest that is earned on top of interest that was previously earned.
Example 2.

Nicholas on the other hand also wants to put his money into an account that earns interest so that he also doesn't have to work to earn money. He, however, would prefer to put his money into an account that earns compound interest instead of simple interest. This way, his money will earn more over time. How much more? Take a look at the table below which illustrates the return Nicholas will receive over the course of 25 years if he puts his money into an account that earns 7% compound interest, again without touching his initial investment.

Interest rate: 7%	Compound interest
Initial deposit	$25,000
Year 1	$26,750
Year 5	$35,063
Year 10	$49,178

Year 15	$68,975
Year 20	$96,472
Year 25	$135,685

As you can see, Nicholas's initial deposit turns into one hundred and thirty-five thousand, six hundred and eighty-five dollars over the course of twenty-five years! That's incredible, it's almost double the amount of his sister's account after twenty-five years.

Example 3.

To put it into a better perspective, let's look at the growth of both Becky and Nicholas's initial deposit side by side.

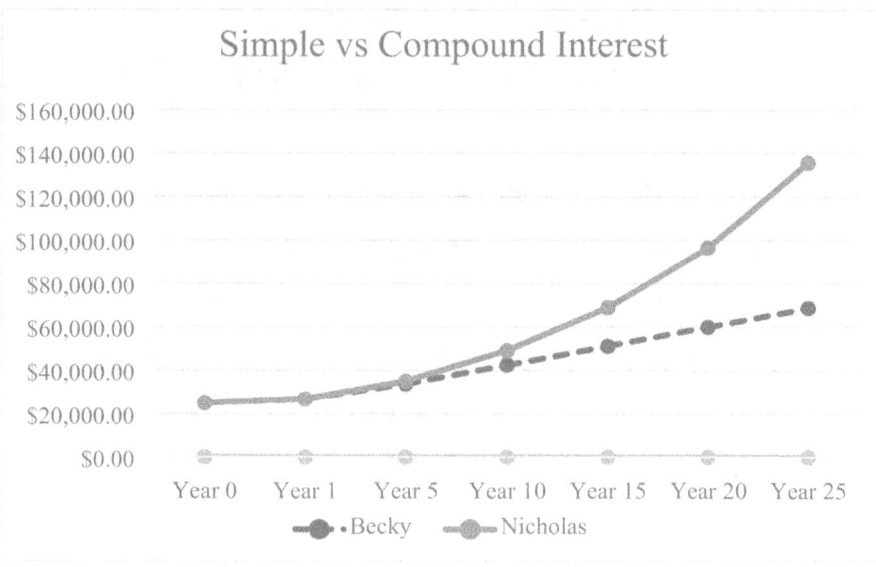

Simple vs Compound Interest

As you can see from the graph above, there isn't much of a difference in the money earned after five years when comparing simple and compound interest. It isn't until year ten where we can clearly notice some separation and see that compounding interest is earning more than simple interest. As time progresses however, you will notice the true power of having your money earn interest on its own interest. Nicholas's account begins to grow almost exponentially while Becky's account remains on a steady upward trend.

Again, the examples given in the previous section show the growth of an initial deposit over time without putting more money in throughout the years. Can you imagine what both accounts may look like if Nicholas and Becky both continuously contribute money to their respective accounts? Twenty-five, fifty, a hundred dollars a month, every month? Their money over time would have the ability to earn even more money! And as you can see from the illustrations and graph, Nicholas's compounding interest account would be able to grow vastly if he decided to continue to put more money in throughout the years. This is one of the very ways the rich wealthy class separate themselves financially from the poor and middle class who can barely afford to get by.

The rich and wealthy understand the concept of compound interest and utilize it to their advantage to exponentially grow their wealth over time. Meanwhile, the poor and middle class utilize compounding to make it harder and harder on themselves to build wealth. How is this possible? As we mentioned in the introduction, we're looking at compound interest from the other side of the coin and how we can earn money. But if we look at compound interest from a consumer perspective, which is 90% of Americans, instead of an investor perspective, consumers will continue to spend more and more money through the use of debt which as we know can be via loans and credit cards. By increasing their debt as time progresses, they PAY interest on a compounding basis, instead of EARN on a compounding basis like an investor. This is a key distinction that can ultimately decide how financially successful you will become.

Consider the tables and graphs given in the previous section to be compounding debt instead of compounding earnings. Can you see how quickly your debt can balloon to huge amounts by allowing it to compound over time? It can literally turn into an amount that's insurmountable to overcome, which unfortunately happens all too often. Again, we hate to sound like a broken record but it's worth mentioning, consumers make their creditors rich while investors make themselves rich. Key in on this distinction and allow this concept to guide your everyday spending. By keeping this concept in mind on a day-by-day basis for every purchase, you will greatly improve your chances of accumulating massive wealth instead of massive debt as time progresses.

Money Myths
"You should allow your money to earn interest, and then use that money you earn in interest to pay for your expenses."
- Ultimately, this should be your goal when you retire. Can you imagine being able to completely live off the interest your money earns, and not having to actually touch your money? Sounds amazing right? But it's completely possible. Using the money you earn on interest early on in your investing career on the other hand can seriously impact your lifetime earnings. To be clear, the money you're earning is your money and is to be used as you please, which can definitely be used to pay for expenses. But if your goal is to accumulate massive wealth it would be in your best interest to continue putting money into your compounding accounts, not take money out.

"When you're young your main priority should be having fun, you'll have plenty of time later to focus on making money and getting your finances together."

- This is true, when you're young you should take advantage of not having the responsibilities you'll have when you're older. You should take the time to learn what your talents are, learn how to monetize your talents, take risks, and learn what strengths and weaknesses you bring to the market. However, you should also be conscious of the fact that compounding becomes increasingly powerful the more time you allow for your money to compound. Again, referring back to our simple and compound interest tables, the end result after twenty-five years illustrates the compound earnings being almost double the amount of the simple interest earnings. Think about how different that would look if it were 30, 35, or 40 years. The difference would be even more significant.

Self-Reflection

1. How can compound interest sabotage your goal of becoming rich or wealthy? What will you do to avoid this from happening?

2. What can you do now, or within the next two years, that would allow you to utilize compound interest to your advantage?

LEARNING HOW TO CREATE ASSETS

"WHEN INDIVIDUALS LEARN HOW TO CREATE ASSETS, THEY HAVE IN ESSENCE, LEARNED HOW TO BUILD THEIR OWN MONEY PRINTING MACHINE."

Having the ability to create and build assets is an invaluable tool you'll need to have in your toolbox if you truly have a desire to be financially successful. To recap, an asset is something that puts money in your wallet every month, and we've already talked about how we can invest in assets such as properties and stocks. What we haven't yet covered however is how we can "create" assets which is a very powerful concept (that again unfortunately isn't taught at all in schools). When individuals learn how to create assets, they have in essence learned how to build their own money printing machine.

It may sound crazy when you first hear it, but what we're really discussing here is creating a product, service, and/or a business. When someone creates a product, service, or a business, what he or she is doing is solving a problem in the marketplace. Where most people see issues and problems, entrepreneurs see opportunities not only to make money but to also help provide solutions for people to solve those issues and problems. The beautiful thing about it is, the more people you can help solve their problems, the more money you can ultimately make! It's a wonderful relationship, but by no means is an easy thing to accomplish (otherwise more people would do it).

Now, the reason why creating assets is such a powerful concept is because before anyone has a real product, service, or business, it all first begins with an idea. Entrepreneurs first see a problem, figure out what the best solution to that problem is, and work tirelessly to make that solution come to life. They're literally taking a thought or idea in their head and making it a real tangible product or service that produces money when customers purchase them (creating something from nothing). Really think about that. Before we all had cell phones, the inventor of cell phones (Martin Cooper) first had to have the idea of creating a cell phone, and then through some sort of trial-and-error process years later had a functional wireless phone in his hand.

Now, we're not saying you have to be the next ultra-genius pioneer that changes the face of technology to be considered an entrepreneur. Not at all, in fact you don't necessarily need to be very smart or have a high IQ (Intelligence Quotient) to succeed as an entrepreneur. It has much more to do with developing the right mindset to see opportunity, problem solving, and having the work ethic to push through until you reach success. In the next section we'll go over some simple examples of problems currently present in the marketplace and how you can capitalize on these opportunities.

Definitions & Examples
Creating: to cause something to come into being. To evolve from a thought or someone's imagination to a work of art or an invention.
Example 1.

Marissa loves to exercise, eat healthy, and stay in good shape. Many of her friends, family, and co-workers always ask her how she is able to maintain such a healthy weight, where she finds the

motivation to exercise so consistently, and what types of food her diet incorporates. Marissa has an entrepreneurial mindset, sees a problem in the marketplace, and figures out a way to help solve this problem utilizing her talents, skills, and knowledge.
- What's the problem: people need help with exercise and nutrition.
- What's the solution: Marissa wants to help as many people as possible exercise regularly and eat healthy food.
- What's the plan: Marissa plans to offer custom meals and exercise plans for customers who are interested via an Instagram page.

Examples 2.

Steve lives in Los Angeles and loves going around the city and eating all sorts of different foods. He eats at Mexican restaurants, Jamaican restaurants, Chinese restaurants, Japanese restaurants, lunch trucks, food carts, hot dog stands, you name it and he's most likely been there. At least once a week Steve makes an effort to go out and try new cuisine. Many of his friends are constantly asking him for recommendations of good places to eat depending on the occasion (anniversary dinners, casual outings, fine dining, brunch, fast food, etc.). Steve is always happy to provide recommendations, but also thinks to himself.... "If only there was a way I can monetize my knowledge of Los Angeles cuisine?" He goes online and realizes people all over the city are constantly commenting on forums and asking the same questions his friends ask him. A light bulb turns on and he sees an opportunity.

- What's the problem: people want to know the best places to eat around the city based on different occasions.

- What's the solution: Steve wants to connect as many people as possible to the cuisines they are looking for in the city.

- What's the plan: Steve is going to begin writing a food blog online sharing his knowledge with the public and monetize his blog by offering restaurants in the city advertising space on his page.

Example 3.

Tiffany is a wine connoisseur (taste specialist) and likes buying bottles of wine to take home after visiting wineries with her husband. She's built a small collection of her favorite wines and will occasionally pop one open on special occasions. One thing she has never enjoyed about opening a bottle of wine, however, is how difficult it can be to actually get the cork out. There are all sorts of different wine bottle opener products available, but none that Tiffany is particularly fond of. She does some quick research online and finds out that people all over the country have the same complaints! She sits and thinks for a few minutes, when all of a sudden, an idea strikes.

- What's the problem: opening a bottle of wine can be a hassle and very difficult.

- What's the solution: have wine bottles come with a lid component pre-attached to the cork allowing for easy removal and eliminating the need of having a wine bottle opener at home.

- What's the plan: develop a working prototype of a lid pre-attached to the cork, get a patent on her product for legal protection, and then sell or license her idea to wineries and wine production companies.

There are literally hundreds, if not thousands of problems just waiting to be solved in the marketplace. Whether it involves creating new products or services that didn't exist before, creating a better way to deliver these products or services, or making improvements on products or services that already exist, the possibilities are truly endless. Consider Instagram for example which Facebook bought back in 2012 for approximately $1 billion dollars. Yes, that's nine zeros which looks like this:

$1,000,000,000

That's a ton of money! Most of you know how to use Instagram and are familiar with most of its features, but do any of you know why Instagram sold for such a huge sum of money? Do any of you know what problems in the marketplace Instagram solves? Does it even solve a problem?

For those of you wondering, here's a short list of things Instagram does better than almost any other application in existence.

1. Instagram created a fast and easy to use platform that allowed users to share photos with friends, which drew a huge amount of people to the application.
2. People are able to follow celebrities, athletes, and influencers whom they admire.
3. People have the ability to build a brand and monetize that brand, for free.

4. Companies who use Instagram are able to promote products to their customers directly.
5. Advertising – brands and companies can use the platform to advertise, form partnerships, and ask for shout outs through industry influencers.

It's estimated that there are more than 1 billion monthly Instagram users in the world. If you view this through a consumer mindset it doesn't mean much, since you mainly care about following and keeping up with friends. But if you view this as an entrepreneur, you would be able to see the incredible amount of value Instagram offers. A billion monthly users really means a billion potential customers for your services or products. Every time someone pulls out their phone and logs onto Instagram is a potential opportunity for you to put your products and services in front of them, which is very valuable.

Are there any issues with Instagram? Of course! No product or service is perfect, which is a great transition to end this section. What tends to happen is that with every new solution that comes to life in the world, two new problems arise. There really will never be a shortage of problems, the real issue lies with people's ability to recognize these problems and lacking the motivation or ability to develop solutions for these problems. Without an entrepreneurial mindset, most individuals will ultimately find it impossible to see the endless amount of opportunity that's present all around them.

Money Myths
"It's impossible to develop an entrepreneurial mindset, you are either born with it or not."
- This is entirely false. Although some individuals are born with the ability to be more creative than others, becoming an entrepreneur has a lot to do with developing the right set of skills. Skills that most of us can acquire through education (self-education not formal education), trial and error, and polishing and refining these skills each day. With continued practice, being an entrepreneur can become second nature in the same way riding a bike is.

"All the problems in the marketplace have already been solved."
- This is also false. As we mentioned before, this is more of a mindset issue than it is a factual issue.

Although there are a lot of great solutions already in existence, the truth is that problems and opportunities exist all around us and will continue to exist even after more solutions have been created. As we mentioned before, every new solution that is developed will bring along with it new problems all requiring their own respective solution.

Self-Reflection

1. What problems or issues do you believe need solving in the world or in your community? Why is it important to solve these problems?

2. How would you solve these problems or issues? How would you monetize your solutions?

ESCAPING THE RAT RACE

"WE ARE NOW ABLE TO DETACH OURSELVES FROM THE DAY-TO-DAY GRIND ALLOWING US TO HAVE THE ULTIMATE AND MOST PRIZED REWARD OF ALL…FREEDOM OF TIME."

Escaping the rat race is widely considered to be the absolute pinnacle of financial success. Very few individuals reach this level, but for those that do often verbalize feelings of overwhelming happiness, relief, and fulfillment. It's a time where individuals can now sit back, relax, and enjoy life for the beautiful gift that it is. They've made the choice to build a solid financial education, got rid of bad debt, have developed multiple streams of income, and chose to buy true assets instead of liabilities. They have enough passive and portfolio income to pay for their monthly expenses, can quit their day job (if they still have one), have completely automated their businesses and investments, and are now able to detach themselves from the day-to-day grind allowing them to have the ultimate and most prized reward of all…. freedom of time.

When we have freedom of time, we have the ability to do things that we truly love to do. Whether that means spending more time with family, traveling the world for months on end, volunteering at shelters and helping those in need, coaching youth sports, reading, writing, exercising, making your vacation home your permanent home, the list can really be endless. We no longer have to spend forty to eighty hours a week working and commuting to pay our bills, we've created wealth and can now afford to do as we please with our time, which is without a doubt our most valuable asset. We can always earn more money by working harder or working smarter, but time is something that we can never earn more of. We only get one chance at life, so why not spend as much time as possible doing the things we truly love doing most?

Definitions & Examples
Rat Race: a comparison between an actual race between rats for the reward of a small piece of cheese and the work life of human beings. Humans will drive long hours to a job that they hate for very little pay and little recognition but will continue to

participate in the never-ending race because their family depends on their paycheck. A common illustration for this is a picture of an employee in a suit running on a hamster wheel.

Example 1.

Gordon and Melinda are in their mid-thirties, live in a suburban area of Denver Colorado, and have two healthy young kids. They both have well-paying jobs making collectively approximately $120,000 dollars per year and live comfortably. On the downside, they have a lot of expenses (babysitting, student loans, rent, groceries, vacations, leisure, etc.), have a difficult time saving money, and although they're paid well by their employers they don't necessarily like their jobs as it often becomes stressful. They greatly look forward to the day they can retire and spend more time together as a family and be more involved in their kids' lives.

Time Freedom: having the ability to spend your time as you please. Work becomes optional, and pursuing your passions full time whether that involves making money or not no longer matters.

Example 2.

Brad and Diana have been married since their early twenties, have two kids in middle school, and live in a suburban area of Las Vegas Nevada. They are now in their late forties, have saved and invested wisely throughout the years, have allowed their savings and investments to compound over time, and now have enough recurring income to quit their job and retire early. Never again having to worry about waking up early, dealing with traffic, asking for permission to take time off work, and begging for raises and bonuses. They are now in complete control of their life and able to get out of the rat race many years sooner than the average working-class individual.

In whose shoes would you rather be, Gordon and Melinda? Or Brad and Diana? The answer should be clear, Brad and Diana are in a much more financially favorable position than Gordon and Melinda. Although Gordon and Melinda have stable jobs that pay them well, they simply can't afford to keep any of the money that they make. It appears as though money flows into their hands, and just as easily as the money flows into their hands it flows right back out due to their expenses. Brad and Diana on the other hand are doing the opposite. When money flows into their hands they pay themselves first by saving and investing, allowing them to keep and multiply the money they make, and then use the money left over after saving and investing to pay for their expenses. Because they were financially savvy, they are now being rewarded with time, money, and options. Meanwhile Gordon and Melinda have no other option but to keep working to pay for their expensive lifestyle.

Although being able to jump off the hamster wheel and escape the rat race may sometimes seem elusive and nearly impossible, it really isn't. It's a matter of yearly, monthly, and daily habits. You must make a conscious effort day in and day out and stick with the process while not focusing solely on the end result. Meaning resisting the temptation to spend money on liabilities, getting into bad debt, and instead focusing on buying and creating assets while minimizing your expenses as much as possible. Will it be easy? No. Will it be difficult? Of course. Will you make mistakes? Everyone does. Will you feel like quitting? Without a doubt. Will it take a lot of time?

Absolutely. But at the end of the day will it be worth it? Only you can be the judge of that. If you sincerely dream about building multiple streams of income, leaving a wealth of assets for your kids and your kid's kids, giving your family a better life, giving yourself and those around you more options, having more time on your hands to spend doing the things you truly love doing, buying your dream home, taking as many vacations as you want, being able to give back to the community, helping those in need...if these are things you've always envisioned yourself doing...then you absolutely must figure out a way to escape from the hamster wheel before you get stuck on it forever.

Money Myths
"I love my job and don't feel a need to escape the rat race."
-If you are passionate about your job, are happy with whom and where you work, and get fulfillment from doing what you do, then who cares about escaping the rat race! Continue working, continue doing what you're doing, and be happy. There's no reason to allow others to change your perspective and lead you

to believe that you're living life the wrong way if you truly are happy.

"It takes too much investment capital to actually be able to escape the rat race."
-It certainly can take a huge investment, in terms of money, time, and effort when it comes to earning enough income to escape the rat race…but it doesn't have to. It's all based on the lifestyle you want. Having a million dollar a year lifestyle is much different than living a one hundred thousand dollar a year lifestyle. The more expenses you intend to have, the more income you'll need to make, which means the more money, time, and effort you'll have to put in to escape the rat race.

Self-Reflection
1. Research investors and entrepreneurs online who have been able to escape the rat race. How were they able to do so?

2. At what age do you plan on escaping the rat race? Outline your plan in doing so.

3. How much recurring income will you need to retire comfortably? What streams of income are you most interested in developing?

FINAL THOUGHTS

You now have a fundamental understanding of the financial roadmap most wealthy individuals use to accumulate their wealth and become successful entrepreneurs, business owners, and investors. It's important to remember that regardless of what phase, stage, or level of the money game you're currently in, you in fact do have what it takes to reach financial freedom and abundance. Never allow fear to be the driving factor that steers you away from making the necessary moves and adjustments you need to make to achieve your goals. Begin to brain wash yourself by forgetting all the self-limiting lies and myths you were told about money and the American Dream growing up, and adopt a new expanding mind set of wealth and abundance. There is an enormous amount of money in the world accessible to anyone that attracts it, no matter the color of your skin or how rough you had it growing up.

On another note, I'm happy to share with you that there is no midterm or final waiting for you after this reading to test how well you memorized the material. Thank god, right? There's a famous quote written by Tom Bodett that's sums this up nicely "In school, you're taught a lesson and then given a test. In life, you're given a test that teaches you a lesson." And it's so very true. Life won't give you any do overs, won't give you any extra credit points or assignments, won't give you extensions on a deadline, won't give you a study guide, and won't assign you a grade of how well you scored on a test. That's simply not the way life works as an adult. As an adult you will make mistakes, you will commit errors, and you will fail, but that's okay. Mistakes and failure are a normal part of becoming successful. This might seem a little radical to most of us because in school and at home we're taught the exact opposite, mistakes and failure are penalized, shameful, and frowned upon. Which is yet again another example of how we weren't given the necessary tools to become financially successful in real life.

I'll leave you with one final thought that's important to consider. Individuals who have accumulated massive amounts of money, assets, and wealth throughout their lifetime always have one single regret... "I wish I would have started sooner." Time is our most valuable asset as it's something we can never get back, so the sooner you start the better! And if we loop this back into our section of Compounding, the more time you allow your money to compound in the market or in investments the more money you will actually make in the long run. Take this into consideration, get started as soon as possible, and turn your dream life into a beautiful reality.

www.ingramcontent.com/pod-product-compliance
Lightning Source LLC
Chambersburg PA
CBHW072152290526
45794CB00004B/1485